Phil H. LISTEMANN

ISBN: 979-1096490-52-3

© 2019 Philedition - Phil Listemann
Colour artwork: Chris Thomas
Layout & project design: Phil Listemann

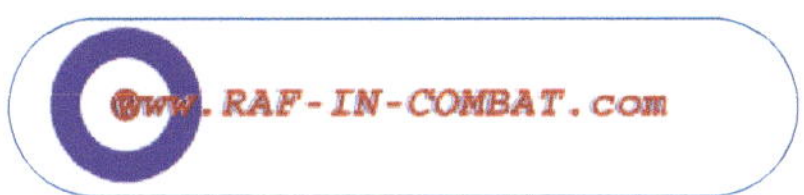

Foreword

The conduct of a successful air campaign requires a combination of strategy, tactics, capable aircraft, well trained pilots - and good leadership.

During WW2, the RAF, Commonwealth (RCAF, RAAF, RNZAF and SAAF) and 'Free European' forces employed almost 250 fighter squadrons throughout the World, from the Aleutians to the South Pacific, throughout Europe, the Middle East and North Africa, India, Burma and the East Indies and East Africa. The RAF's basic tactical formation was the squadron, and this was the first step of independent commanders usually held by a Squadron Leader. The period in command could vary from a matter of days to over a year and so many hundreds of men were appointed as Officers Commanding (OC) of a squadron. As tactics developed and larger formations were used in action, several squadrons would operate in concert and were grouped together as a Wing, led by a Wing Leader. usually of Wing Commander rank. By the mid war years as these Wings became independent mobile formations, the command was given to a Group Captain with leadership in the air held by the Wing Leader, more formally titled as Wing Commander Flying (WingCo). Most were highly decorated, and some were very successful aces but all were highly experienced with a proven record of leadership and ability.

The aim of this series is to introduce these men so far as available information allows by giving short biography and describing the operational units that they led during the war.

Acknowledgement:
André Bar, Steve Brew, Hugh Haliday, Michael Schoeman, Paul Sortehaug,
Andrew Thomas, Chris Thomas, Pavel Vancata.

The range of military decoration for airmen during the war was large, and this is not the aim here to recall of them. The Victoria Cross was the highest award, but only one fighter pilot had had the honour to receive it over the 32 Victoria Crosses awarded during WW2. However, some were regulary awarded to airmen, and specifically to the fighter leaders.

The **Victoria Cross (VC)** is Britain's highest military honour. First instituted by Queen Victoria during the Crimean War in 1856, the VC is awarded for "*most conspicuous bravery, or some daring or pre-eminent act of valour or self-sacrifice, or extreme devotion to duty in the presence of the enemy*." The bronze cross is cast from Russian guns captured at Sevastapol. In the century and a half since its creation, 1 351 have been awarded and only three bars.

The **Distinguished Service Order (DSO)**, is open to officers of all services, and was awarded from 1886 for "*distinguished services during active operations against the enemy*." From 1917 this specifically required action under fire. The order is generally given to officers in command above the rank of Flight Lieutenant/1st Lieutenant and awards to ranks below this are usually for a high degree of gallantry just short of deserving the Victoria Cross.

The **Distinguished Flying Cross** (DFC) is a military decoration awarded to personnel of the United Kingdom's Royal Air Force and other services, and formerly to officers of other Commonwealth countries, for "*an act or acts of valour, courage or devotion to duty whilst flying in active operations against the enemy*".
The award was established on 3 June 1918, shortly after the formation of the RAF. A DFC can be awarded to a steady, rock solid, dependable pilot, or one who has shown noticeable growth and improvement over a period of time.
During the Second World War, 20,354 DFCs were awarded, the most of any award, with approximately 1,550 first bars and 45 second bars. Honorary awards were made on 964 occasions to aircrew from other non-commonwealth countries.

The **Distinguished Flying Medal** (DFM) was until 1993 a military decoration awarded to personnel of the Royal Air Force (United Kingdom) and the other services, and formerly also to personnel of other Commonwealth countries, below commissioned rank, for "*an act or acts of valour, courage or devotion to duty whilst flying in active operations against the enemy*".
The medal was established on 3 June 1918. It was the other ranks' equivalent to the Distinguished Flying Cross, which was awarded to commissioned officers and Warrant Officers (although WOs could also be awarded the DFM), although it ranked below the DFC in order of precedence, between the Military Medal and the Air Force Medal. In 1993 the DFM was discontinued, and since then the Distinguished Flying Cross has been awarded to personnel of all ranks.
During World War II, 6,637 DFMs were awarded, with 60 first award bars and a unique second bar. Some 165 were awarded to aircrew from other non- Commonwealth countries.

List of pilots - Volume II

W.S. **Arthur** (Aus)

A. **Austeen** (Nor)

E.R. **Baker** (UK)

L.H. **Bartlett** (UK)

R.P. **Beamont** (UK)

R.W. **Bungey** (Aus)

W.M. **Churchill** (UK)

W.G. **Clouston** (NZ)

A.M. **Colenbrander** (SA)

L.F. DE **Soomer** (Bel)

H.J. **Dowding** (Can)

B. **Drake** (UK)

M. **Duryasz** (Pol)

J.F. **Edwards** (Can)

J.M. **Faure** (SA)

E.F.M.L. **Fayolle** (Fr)

R.H.M. **Gibbes** (Aus)

D.E. **Gillam** (UK)

H.C. **Godefroy** (Can)

R.K. **Hayward** (NFL)

Z. **Henneberg** (Pol)

E. **Holden** (UK)

E. **Horbaczewski** (Pol)

C.B. **Hull** (SR)

K.E. **James** (Aus)

S.I. **Kellas** (Gr)

J.R.C. **Kilian** (NZ)

F. **Kornicki** (Pol)

O.L. **Kucera** (Cz)

J.J. **Le Roux** (SA)

R.F.F.G. **Malengreau** (Bel)

J. **Manak** (Cz)

R.L.. **Mannix** (USA)

R.D. **May** (Aus)

H.W. **McLeod** (Can)

H.O. **Mehre** (Nor)

H de M. **Molson** (Can)

D.G. **Morris** (UK)

R.L. **Morrison** (SA)

T.F. **Neil** (UK)

J.B.E. **Nicolson** (UK)

H.H. **Norsworthy** (Can)

C.G. **Peterson** (USA)

J. **Sample** (UK)

J.H. **Schloesing** (Fr)

D.H. **Seaton** (UK)

R. VAN **Lierde** (Bel)

A. **Vasatko** (Cz)

R.G. **Watts** (NZ)

E.P. **Wells** (NZ)

V.J. **Wheeler** (UK)

W.T.F. **Wightman** (UK)

Squadron Leader
pennant

Wing Commander
pennant
(WingCo flying)

Group Captain
pennant
(OC Wing - Non flying or Station commander)

ARTHUR,
Wilfred Stanley,
RAAF

Aus. 565

Australian

DSO, DFC

'Woof' Arthur, from Queensland, Australia, enlisted as a regular officer in the RAAF when the war broke out. In December 1939 he was serving with No. 22 Squadron RAAF but was posted to No. 3 Squadron in the Middle East three months later. He would remain with this unit until August 1941. He first flew Gladiators and claimed his first successes on 12 December 1940 when he destroyed two Italian aircraft and damaged one. In 1941 he made more claims, now flying Hurricanes, before being posted for a rest as a flight instructor at No. 71 OTU. In January 1942 he was awarded a DFC and was repatriated to Australia in March. He was posted to No. 76 Squadron RAAF in April but instead went to No. 2 OTU two weeks later. In January 1943 he was given command of **No. 75 Squadron RAAF** with which he claimed a 'Betty' bomber on 10 March. In June, having just been awarded an immediate DSO for his action of 14 April, when he continued to lead and fight against a Japanese force despite having no guns capable of firing, he was posted as Wing Leader of **No. 71 Wing RAAF**. Here he made his last claim, a probable 'Betty' on 31 October 1943 to bring his total to eight confirmed victories, two probables and six damaged. In November, his tour expired, he was sent back for a rest and was promoted to Group Captain at the age of 24. He started another tour, in December 1944, as CO of **No. 81 Wing** then, in April, took command of **No. 78 Wing**. Arthur left the RAAF in February 1946.

Curtiss P-40E A29-143 at the time when 'Woof' Arthur was commanding 75 Sqn RAAF. This squadron was the first to be formed in Australia on the P-40 and received its first machines in March 1942 before being rushed to Port Moresby, New Guinea, to defend against the Japanese. A29-143 was destroyed, and its pilot killed, on 8 August 1943 during a low-level aerobatics flight.
(AHM of WA).

AUSTEEN,
Arne,
RNAF

N. 1127

Norwegian

DFC

Arne Austeen was trained as a pilot in the Norwegian Army Air Service before studying to become a mechanical engineer at Trondheim and graduating in 1938. Austeen briefly took part in the fighting against the German invasion of April 1940. Early in 1941, he decided to flee to Sweden in skis and from there he travelled to Moscow, Vladisvostok, Japan and California before reaching 'Little Norway' which was near Toronto in Canada in July 1941.

He was retrained as a fighter pilot and, on completion of his training, was posted to the UK and No. 124 Squadron in November 1941 before moving to No. 332 (Norwegian) Squadron in January 1942 and then No. 64 Squadron in March. It is with this unit that he opened his score with the shared destruction of an Fw190 on 30 July. In January 1943 his tour expired and he served as a gunnery instructor. He joined No. 611 (West Lancashire) Squadron, in August 1943, as a flight commander for his second tour of operations. Before the year was out he had made more claims to bring his total to six confirmed victories, one being shared, and three aircraft damaged. He made his claims on 24 October. In January 1944 he was also awarded the DFC. The previous October he had been posted to **No. 331 (Norwegian) Squadron** to take over the squadron and he stayed there until the end of his tour in March 1944. He spent a year as Chief Instructor at the Central Gunnery School before starting a third tour in February 1945 as OC of **No. 126 Squadron** flying Mustang Mk.IIIs. He led this unit until 4 May 1945 when his aircraft, KH578/5J-B, was hit by flak from the U-boats he was strafing. It blew up and Austeen sadly became the last Norwegian pilot to be killed during WW2.

No. 126 Sqn transitioned to the Mustang late in the war, in December 1944, and did not have the opportunity to make many claims. Only two were made before the end of war but one of those was an Me262.
(MJF Bowyer, via A. Thomas).

BAKER,
Ernest Reginald, RAF

RAF **No. 40660**

British

DSO, DFC & Bar

'Reg' Baker, the son of a coal miner, joined the RAF in May 1938. He joined No. 210 Squadron flying Short Sunderlands, and when war broke out developed a highly successful strategy for attacking U-Boats, sinking three and earning him his first DFC in November 1940. In the autumn of 1941 he attended a Specialist Navigation Course in Canada and returned to 210 Sqn now flying Catalina's. In May 1942 he was posted to India to join No. 240 Squadron, but en-route crash-landed in Malta. Declared unfit to fly with Operational Stress, he was grounded for 8 months. Converting to fighters in late 1942, he then joined No. 182 Squadron flying Hawker Typhoons in a ground attack role until June 1943. Promoted to Squadron Leader, he was posted to command **No. 263 Squadron**, flying Westland Whirlwinds, and in October 1943 was awarded his second DFC for a daring low level attack on the German Ore Carrier 'Munsterland' in bad visibility in Cherbourg Harbour, scoring a direct hit. Promoted to Wing Commander in 1944 and in April, he became the Wing Leader of the **No. 146 Airfield** (later **Wing** from 12 May 1944), flying Typhoons and leading the Wing on many successful raids over Northern France, both before and after D-Day. It was on 16th June 1944 that his good luck eventually ran out whilst leading an attack on German positions holding three important River Bridges. After being hit by intense flack, his Typhoon MN754 dived towards the ground, crashing in an orchard at St Mauvieu in Normandy. He was awarded the DSO the day of his death.

When 'Reg' Baker took command of No. 263 Sqn, the Squadron was the last Whirlwind unit of the RAF in active service. The Whirlwind was at time used in the fighter-bomber role. It was withdrawn from the operation in December in the same time Baker left 263 Sqn. Baker conducted the last Whirlwind operation of the war on 29 November, an attempt to destroy mine-sweepers Junkers Ju52s off Cherbourg.

'Red' or 'Len' Bartlett joined the RAF in June 1939 as an airman pilot. He completed his training and joined a Hurricane unit, No. 17 Squadron, in July 1940 as an NCO. He was just in time to participate in the Battle of Britain. He opened his score on 28 August by sharing in the destruction of a Ju88. Over the following weeks he made more claims and by the end of 1940 his tally had reached three confirmed victories, one being shared, and three probables (one also shared). On 18 March 1941 he was shot down and wounded but returned to the squadron at the end of July after receiving a commission. In February 1942 he was posted to No. 137 Squadron, a Whirlwind unit, with which he claimed a Ju88 as damaged on 6 July. In September he received a promotion and was posted to a Hurricane fighter unit, **No. 253 Squadron**, as OC. With this unit he participated in the landings in North Africa in November 1942 and made his final claim on 10 January 1943 when he destroyed a Ju88. He remained with the squadron until January 1944 and received the DSO two months later. No further operational positions followed before the end of the war. Bartlett served with the RAF after the war and was one of the six Group Captains chosen to represent the RAF at Winston Churchill's funeral. He retired in 1966.

Hurricane Mk. I N2359 of 17 Sqn during the Battle of Britain. Len Bartlett made most of his claims when he was serving with this squadron during the Battle of Britain. The squadron claimed about 60 German aircraft destroyed or probably destroyed during this period.

BEAMONT,
Roland Prosper,
RAF

RAF **No. 41819**

British

DSO & Bar, DFC & Bar

'Bee' Beamont joined the RAF on a short service commission in January 1939. On completion of his training he was posted to France and joined No. 87 Squadron on Hurricanes. Action came with the launch of the German offensive in May and Beamont made his first claim on the 13th, a Do17 destroyed, before making further claims on the 14th, 15th and 17th. He continued to fly with the squadron during the Battle of Britain and, at 19, was one of youngest pilots of Fighter Command when the battle began. He achieved more successes in August with three confirmed victories, two more probables and two aircraft damaged. He was awarded the DFC in June 1941 and was posted soon after to No. 79 Squadron, again on Hurricanes, as a flight commander. He remained with the unit until December but was unable to add to his score. He then became a test pilot at Hawker's. He returned to operations with No. 56 Squadron in May 1942 before joining **No. 609 Squadron** in June. This unit had recently converted to the Hawker Typhoon and he took command in October. He would remain at the head of the squadron until May 1943. By that time he had received a Bar to his DFC, in January 1943, a DSO in May and had claimed one Ju88 damaged at night. He then returned to Hawker's as a test pilot. In February 1944 he started a new tour and was given WingCo flying position of a Typhoon wing, **No. 150 Wing** which would become the first Tempest wing in spring. He led the Wing during D-Day but, soon after, he was called upon to hunt the V-1s. Flying Tempests, he destroyed 31 of them (five shared) before the end of August and ended the hunt with a Bar to his DSO awarded in July. He moved with his Wing to the Continent and made his last claim on 2 October, an Fw190 destroyed, to bring his total to ten confirmed victories (one shared), two probables and four damaged. However, his war ended ten days later when he was shot down by flak (flying Tempest EJ710) and became a PoW. After the war, after leaving the RAF, he continued his career as test pilot.

The Spitfires of 609 Sqn gave way Typhoons in May 1942. It would be the only fighter squadron to make this conversion as the Typhoon units were usually former Hurricane squadrons. The Typhoon would be flown by 609 until the end of war.

**Hawker Tempest Mk V EJ706, W/C R.P. Beamont,
No. 150 Wing, B.80 Volkel, Netherlands, October 1944**

Bungey,
**Robert Wilton,
RAF & RAAF**

RAF No. 40042 &
Aus. 257414

Australian

DFC

Bungey was from South Australia and first trained with the RAAF in 1936. After he graduated he was temporarily transferred to the RAF on a short service commission and embarked for England on the 22 July 1937. After further training he was posted to No. 226 Squadron which had just received its first Fairey Battles. He joined the AASF in France in September 1939 and participated in the Battle of France. On his return to the UK, he responded, in August 1940, to a call for volunteers for Fighter Command and joined No. 145 Squadron in September.

He stayed with the squadron until March 1941. By that time he had become a flight commander and, during the last six months, he claimed the destruction of two enemy aircraft (both being shared) and had damaged another.

He left the squadron for medical reasons, his knee needing surgery but after recovery he was posted as OC of **No. 452 (RAAF) Squadron** in June and remained in this position until January 1942. He made his last claim, a Bf109 destroyed, on 6 December. He left his command with a DFC that was awarded in October 1941. From that point Bungey took various staff positions before being transferred to Australia in January 1943. He arrived in May and was transferred back to the RAAF at the same time. He was stationed with No. 2 OTU in Mildura as acting Wing Commander but died in tragic circumstances on 10 June 1943.

During the months from the summer of 1941 to March 1942, 452 Sqn became one of the most successful fighter squadrons in Fighter Command. The Spitfire Mk.V (here BM514/UD-A) was introduced to the squadron in August and 54 German aircraft were claimed as destroyed or probably destroyed before the squadron was sent for a rest. *(Bill Maudlin via Drew Harrison)*

CHURCHILL,
Walter Myers,
RAF

AAF **No. 90241**

British

DSO, DFC

Walter Churchill joined the Auxiliary Air Force in 1931 and commissioned with
No. 605 (County of Warwick) Squadron in 1932. In 1937 he went on to the Reserve of Officers and was recalled to
full-time service with the squadron in August 1939. In November he was posted to **No. 3 Squadron** as a flight commander and followed the unit to France in May 1940. He made his first, and only, claims during the Battle of France
and returned to Britain with six confirmed victories (two being shared) and two inconclusive (the term 'probable' would
be used later). When the CO was killed in action on 16 May, he took command of the squadron. By the end of May the
squadron was withdrawn to Kenley and Churchill had been awarded both the DSO and the DFC. In June he was posted
to his former unit as OC and participated in the Battle of Britain. At the end of September he left 605 to become the
first OC of **No. 71 (Eagle) Squadron** (the first fighter unit to be manned by American pilots). However, due to a
recurrent sinus problem, he had to relinquish his command in January 1941 and remained grounded for a period. Fit
again for operational flying, he was posted overseas as a Group Captain, in July 1942, to command RAF Takali in Malta
where furious combats were engaged. He flew a Spitfire off the aircraft carrier HMS *Furious* on 11 August 1942 and landed
on Malta. He planned the first offensive sweeps over Sicily on the 23rd and, four days later while leading the second one, his
Spitfire, EP339, crashed in flames after being hit by flak. There was no chance of
survival for Churchill.

When 71 (Eagle) Sqn was formed,
the RAF was going to equip it with
Brewster Buffalos inherited from
the Belgians. Walter Churchill cam-
paigned against this and eventually the squadron received
Hurricanes and became operational early in 1941 shortly after the
departure of Churchill for health
problems.

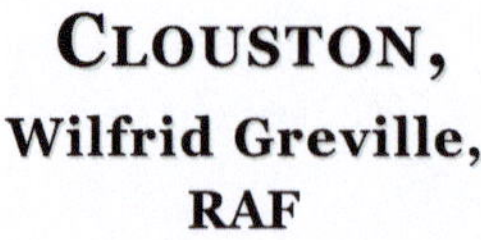

CLOUSTON,
Wilfrid Greville, RAF

RAF No. 39223

New Zealander

DFC

'Wilf' Clouston joined the RAF on a short service commission in March 1936 and on completion of training, he joined No. 19 Squadron in May 1937. The unit was equipped with Gloster Gauntlet bi-planes , but the following year became the first in the RAF to update with Spitfires. Shortly after the outbreak of war in September 1939, he was made a flight commander, and saw action during the Battle of France and then Battle of Britain. He made his first claim on 11 May 1940, sharing the destruction of a Ju88 and towards the end of June, by which time he had accumulated a further five confirmed victories, was awarded the DFC. During the Battle of Britain, he made more claims, the last on 18 September, bringing his score to eleven confirmed victories, three being shared, two probably destroyed, one being shared, and a share in damaging another aircraft. His leadership and experience saw him promoted and in November 1940 he was given the task of forming **No. 258 Squadron** flying Hurricanes. He was shot down and slightly wounded on one occasion and continued to lead this squadron until August 1941. He was then selected and posted out to Singapore where during October 1941 he oversaw the working up to operational status of **No. 488 (NZ) Squadron** on Brewster Buffaloes. Towards the end of January 1942, he relinquished command of the unit going into the Operations Room at HQ RAF Singapore. He escaped from Singapore mid-February, but was captured at sea making for Java. Liberated in September 1945, he obtained a permanent commission with the RAF until ill-health forced him to retire in 1956.

A Brewster Buffalo of No. 488 (NZ) Sqn at dispersal at Kallang in Singapore. The squadron was the last Buffalo unit on Singapore to become operational. It fought courageously over the island, but its losses outstripped its successes. 488 Squadron was re-equipped with Hurricanes, and after the fall of Singapore and the Dutch East Indies, was reformed in the UK as a night fighter squadron.

COLENBRANDER,
Adrian Montague, SAAF

SAAF **No. P102667V**

South African

-

Adrian Colenbrander joined the South African Permanent Force before the war. When the war broke out, he was serving at the South African Military College. In May 1940 he was posted to No. 1 Squadron SAAF to fly Gladiators. In June and July 1940 he was attached to No. 112 Squadron RAF before returning to his unit in October 1940 and fighting against the Italians in Eastern Africa. On 14 August, while on patrol, he managed to damage a Ca133 that was attacking his landing strip. This was the first SAAF Gladiator engagement. He was then posted to No. 2 Squadron SAAF between October 1940 and April 1941.

In July 1942 he was posted to Western Africa and **No. 2 Squadron SAAF** to fly Kittyhawks. He took command of the squadron in the following month. On 11 November 1942, during a combat, the squadron would claim eight Stukas destroyed and four probable. Colenbrander claimed one probable (and possibly a second that has alternatively been credited to him or the squadron as a whole). One week later, on 13 November, Colenbrander led 2 Squadron on a mission to strafe a road along Gazala-Tmini but was hit by ground fire, hit the sea at high speed and was killed in his Kittyhawk Mk.I (EV360).

A 1 Sqn Gladiator, stationed in Northern Kenya, ready to take off to intercept any Italian raid. This Squadron claimed 22 Italian aircraft destroyed or probably destroyed while flying Gladiators.
(M. Schoeman)

De Soomer,
Léon Frans, RAF

RAF No. 61935

Belgian

DFC

De Soomer served with the *Belgian Aéronautique Militaire* (Military Aviation) as a regular officer and pilot before the war and, when Belgium was invaded in May 1939, was serving as a Captain in a HQ position.

When Belgium capitulated, he managed to flee in England in June 1940. He joined the Belgian forces stationed there and became the Air Attaché in the United Kingdom. In the search of action, he decided to enlist in the RAF in March 1941 and in June he was posted to No. 32 Squadron to fly Hurricanes. In May 1942 he was posted to No. 174 Squadron as a flight commander and participated in the operation over Dieppe where the squadron lost five Hurricanes. However, soon after, he was given the command of **No. 3 Squadron** and transitioned from the Hurricane to the Hawker Typhoon during the following February. He relinquished his command in August 1943 and a DFC was awarded in September. He then served in various HQ positions until the end of war.

De Soomer continued to serve with the new Belgian Air Force, reaching the rank of Major-General, and once more became the Air Attaché in Great Britain.

Typhoon EJ922 was one of the first Typhoons to be issued to 3 Sqn when it converted to the type. De Soomer supervised all of the training and led the squadron's first Typhoon operation on 16 May 1943.
(C.W.Cain via C. Thomas)

Harry Dowding, from Ontario, Canada, joined the RCAF in March 1941. He started his training in Canada and completed it in the UK in June 1942 after attending an OTU course. He was then posted to No. 403 (RCAF) Squadron as an NCO. He remained with the unit for more than a year during which he was commissioned and made various claims. The first was on 13 May when he claimed a Bf109 destroyed off Le Touquet in France. When he left the squadron in October 1943 he had added five more (three being shared) along with two damaged. He was also awarded a DFC the same month.

In March 1944 he was posted to **No. 442 (RCAF) Squadron** for his second tour of operations as a flight commander before taking over the squadron in July. A couple of days before assuming command, he had made his last claims, with two confirmed Bf109s on 27 June and one Fw190 damaged the next day, to bring his total to eight confirmed victories (three being shared), and three damaged aircraft. At the end of September he relinquished his command and was repatriated to Canada, receiving a Bar to his DFC in December. He was released from the RCAF in February 1945.

A pair of 442 Sqn Spitfires IXs (MK454/Y2-Y leading MK777/Y2-Z) taking off from an airfield in Normandy in early August 1944. During the war 442 was responsible for the destruction of 53 enemy aircraft with five more being accounted for as probably destroyed.
(Donald Nijboer)

DRAKE,
Billy,
RAF

RAF **No. 39095**

British

DSO, DFC & Bar

Billy Drake joined the RAF in July 1936. He was first posted to No. 1 Squadron at the time the squadron was flying Hawker Furies but soon converted to Hurricanes. This squadron moved to France at the outbreak of war and Drake saw action there and made his first claims on 20 April with a Bf109 confirmed and another one unconfirmed. He participated in the Battle of France and made more claims but was shot down and wounded. At the end of October, after a full recovery, he was sent to No. 213 Squadron but soon volunteered to serve with the newly-formed Spitfire No. 421 Flight. This was a low-level reconnaissance unit with which he added more German aircraft to his tally and, in January 1941, he was awarded the DFC. Shortly after the flight became No. 91 (Nigeria) Squadron, Drake became a flight commander and was posted out for a rest. In September 1941 he was posted to Western Africa to command **No. 128 Squadron** under formation (the mission being to intercept French aircraft intruding over the region). While there he obtained a rare victory over a French aircraft on 13 December. He was posted to the Western Desert in April 1942 and took command of **No. 112 Squadron**, flying Kittyhawks, during the next month. With this unit he would make most of his claims (24). He added a Bar to his DFC in July and followed that with a DSO in December. In January, he was posted away having attained the rank of Wing Commander. In June 1943 he was posted to Malta to become the Wing Leader of the **Krendi Wing** and remained in this role until October. There, he made his last claim on 7 July, a MC202 destroyed over Italy, to bring his tally to 25 confirmed victories (three being shared), seven probable or unconfirmed victories (one shared) and six aircraft damaged, one being shared. He returned to the UK where he served as Wing Leader of **No. 136 Airfield** on Typhoons for five months between December 1943 and April 1944. This was his last operational posting before the end of war. Drake remained with the RAF until retirement in July 1963.

Number 128 Sqn (code 'WG') was kind of unique as it was formed in 1941 to counter the French who regularly sent reconnaissance aircraft over the British West African colony. One French aircraft was shot down in December 1941.

Hawker Hurricane Mk.IIB/Trop. BD897, S/L Billy Drake, Hastings, Sierra Leone, December 1941.

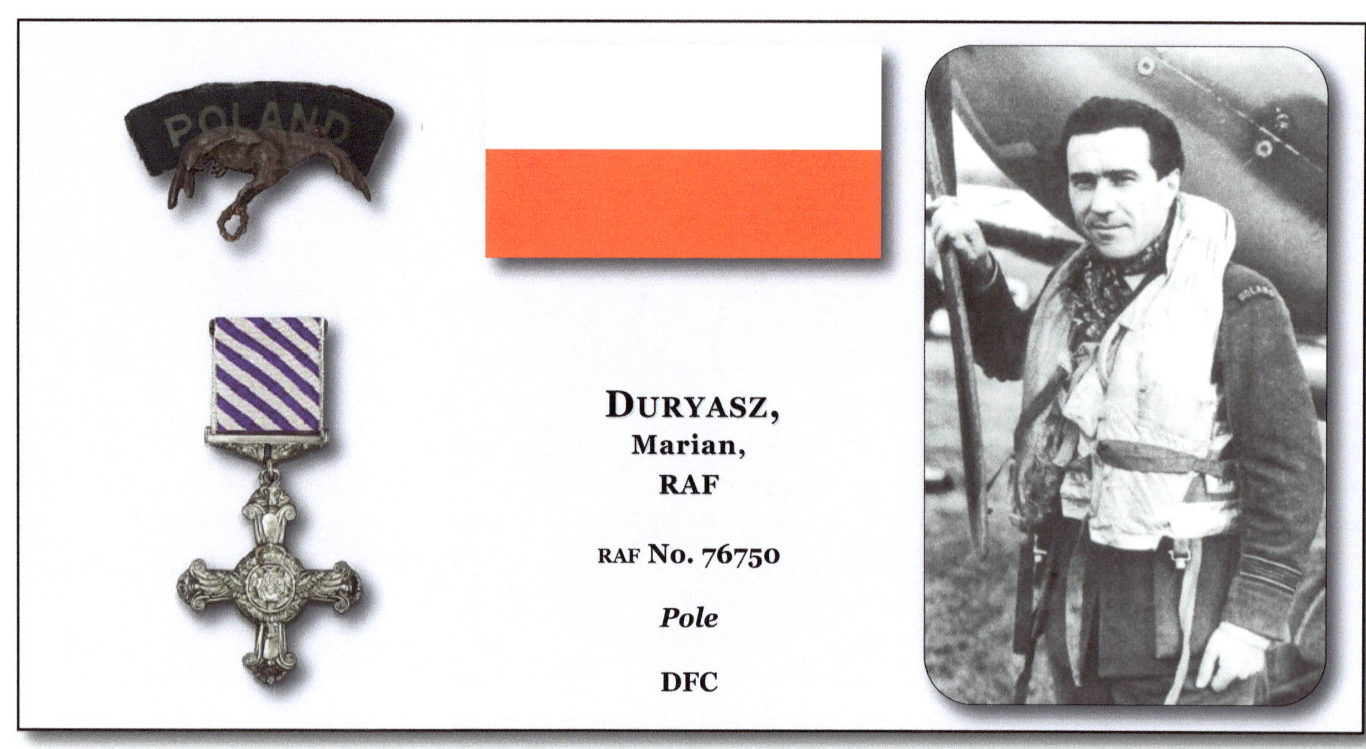

DURYASZ, Marian, RAF

RAF **No. 76750**

Pole

DFC

Marian Duryasz enlisted in the Polish Air Force in 1932. In September 1939 he was a pilot instructor at the Advanced Flying Training School at Ulez. Along with many other instructors, when the Germans launched their offensive, he was rushed into a newly-formed unit called the Deblin Fighter Group and participated in the short Polish campaign. He escaped to France via Romania and, in January 1940, to the UK where he was re-trained. In August 1940 he was posted to No. 213 Squadron in the middle of the Battle of Britain. He opened his score on 11 September with a Bf110 claimed as destroyed and followed that with a Do17 on the 15th and a probable He111 on the 26th. In October he was posted to the recently formed No. 302 (Polish) Squadron in an Operations Room role that did not allow him to fly much. In February 1941 he was posted to No. 317 (Polish) Squadron, under formation, and became a flight commander during the following month. He remained with 317 until June 1942 but made his last claim on 28 April 1942 (a Fw190). His tally now stood at three confirmed victories and one probably destroyed aircraft.

A new tour started in June 1943, first with No. 316 (Polish) Squadron, then with **No. 302 (Polish) Squadron** again in January 1944 before moving again to No. 308 (Polish) Squadron in May. In July, however, he returned to 302 to take command of the unit he would lead until the end of his tour in January 1945. He left with a DFC awarded in October 1944. Duryasz returned to Poland in 1947 and continued to serve with the new Polish Air Force even though he was expelled by the Communists between 1950 and 1957.

No. 302 Sqn switched to the Spitfire Mk.IX in September 1943 and MH869/WX-R had just been issued to the unit when Duryasz arrived in January 1944. The squadron is credited with 82 confirmed or probable aircraft destroyed during the war but only four of these were claimed while flying the Mk.IX.
(Wilhelm Ratuszynski)

EDWARDS,
James Francis,
RCAF

CAN./ J.1607

Canadian

DFC & Bar, DFM

'Eddie' Edwards, from Saskatchewan, joined the RCAF in October 1940. In July 1941 he sailed to the UK as an NCO and, after the completion of his course at No. 55 OTU, was sent to the Middle East. In January 1942 he was posted to No. 94 Squadron, flying Kittyhawks, where he made his first two claims in March (2nd and 23rd). Edwards moved to No. 260 Squadron in May and during the next twelve months would meet with considerable success. At the end of the Tunisian campaign his tally had risen to fifteen confirmed victories (three being shared), he had been awarded the DFM and the DFC within four days, and was a respected flight commander. His tour ended in May 1943.

He started another tour in November in Italy with No. 417 (RCAF) Squadron on Spitfires before moving, in December, to No. 92 Squadron as a flight commander (also flying Spitfires). With this unit he made several further claims especially over Anzio in Italy. In March 1944 he was appointed OC of **No. 274 Squadron** and moved with the unit to the UK soon afterwards. He led the squadron equipped with Spitfires during the Battle of Normandy and converted to the Tempest before becoming tour-expired in August and relinquishing his command. He received a Bar to his DFC two months later. He returned to operations a final time in March 1945 as Wing Commander Flying of

No. 127 (RCAF) Wing. He led this unit until the end of war. At the head of the wing, he made his last claim on 3 May 1945 when he shared in the destruction of a Ju88 and brought his tally to eighteen confirmed victories (three being shared), nine probable (one being shared) and thirteen damaged. He remained with the RCAF until 1972.

By the end of 1942 260 Sqn had just been re-equipped with the Kittyhawk Mk.III. Edwards, at that time, was flying FR350/HS-B with which he claimed two confirmed victories on 30 December (one being shared). The squadron claimed over 90 confirmed and probable victories between February 1942 and the end of the Tunisian campaign.

FAURE,
Johannes Morkel, SAAF

SAAF No. 143113V

South African

DSO, DFC & Bar

'Hannes' Faure joined the SA Artillery Regiment in June 1940 before enlisting to the SAAF in August. On completion of his training he was posted to No. 71 OTU in Sudan for service in the Western Desert. He was posted to No. 1 Squadron SAAF in January 1942, flying Hurricanes, and made his first two 'kills' on 23 July against Ju87s. In August he was attached to No. 92 Squadron as an acting flight commander with the specific aim to become familiar with the Spitfire as 1 Squadron was scheduled to receive the Spitfire in the near future. While with 92, he claimed one Bf109 destroyed and one more damaged before returning to his unit in September. Still flying Hurricanes, he claimed two Ju87s on 2 November, including one probable, but was shot down two days later. He managed to walk back to his unit and scored once more on the 27th (a Bf109) but flying a Spitfire this time. His tour ended in December 1942 and he returned to the Union and was posted to No. 6 Squadron SAAF between January and June 1943. He was awarded the DFC in March. In June 1943 he returned to **No. 1 Squadron SAAF** for another tour. Now flying the Spitfire Mk.IX, he made his last claim on 19 July when he shared in the destruction of an Fw190. His score was now five confirmed victories, one probable and one damaged. The same month, he was given command of the squadron and relinquished it in February 1944 at the end of his second tour. After a short period as a flying instructor in South Africa, he was again sent to Italy for a third tour, as OC **No. 4 Squadron SAAF**, between July and November 1944. He was promoted to Lieutenant Colonel and became WingCo Flying of **No. 324 Wing** until VE-Day leaving for South Africa soon after. In February 1945, he was awarded the DSO and, in May 1945, he added a Bar to his DFC. Faure continued to serve in the SAAF until 1950.

No. 1 Sqn SAAF was among the first of the fighter squadrons in North Africa to be re-equipped with Spitfire Mk.Vs. The conversion took place in November 1942 just before Faure left. This Spitfire Mk.V (EP649) was one of the first Spitfires taken on charge by the South Africans. The squadron would claim over 30 aircraft destroyed or probably destroyed by the end of the campaign for Tunisia in May 1943.

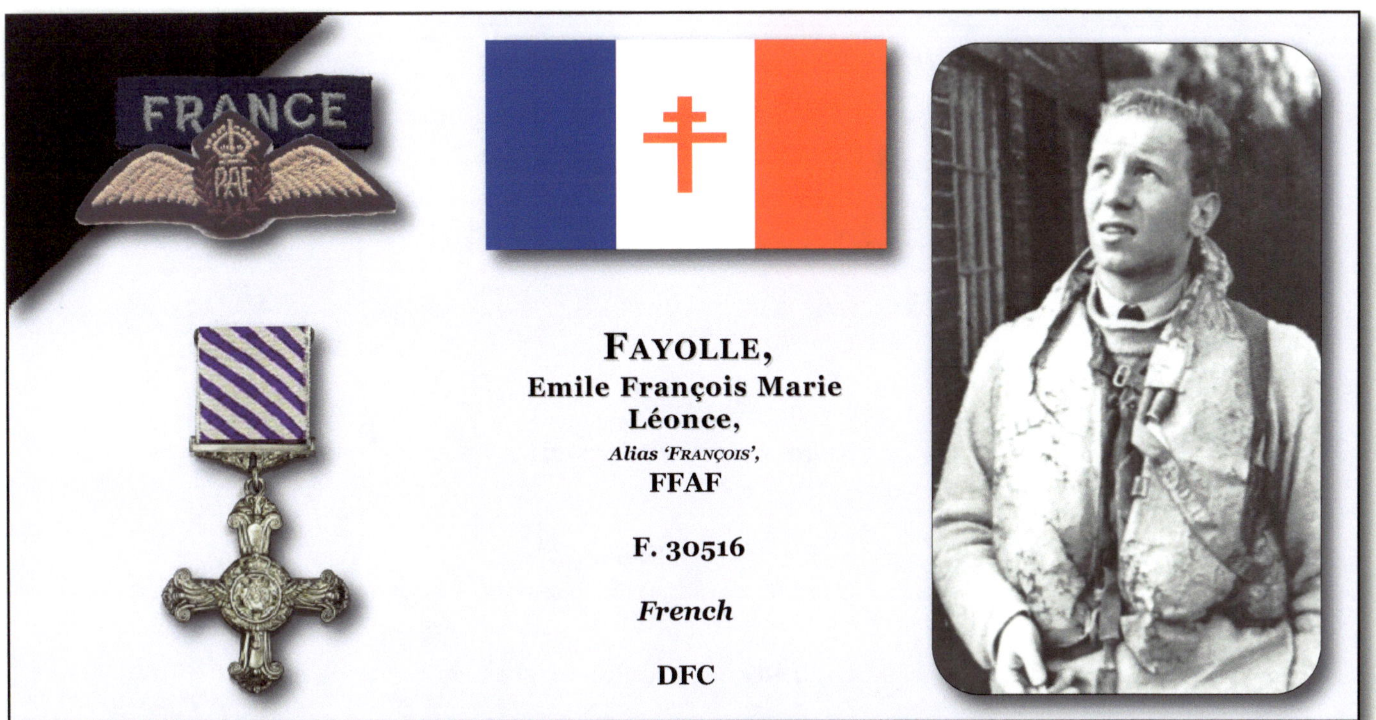

FAYOLLE,
Emile François Marie Léonce,
Alias 'François',
FFAF

F. 30516

French

DFC

Emile Fayolle, the son of a French Admiral, enlisted in the French Air Force as an NCO in November 1938 to become a fighter pilot. In June 1940 he was at the end of his training in North Africa and, in the hope of continuing the struggle against Germany, escaped to Gibraltar by stealing a liaison aircraft with a friend. He arrived in England in July and enlisted in the new Free French Air Force where he took the nickname 'François'. Because his training was almost completed, he was quickly retrained by the RAF and, in September 1940, joined No. 85 Squadron to become one of the thirteen Frenchmen to be engaged in the Battle of Britain. In December 1940 he was posted to No. 145 Squadron and then No. 242 (Canadian) Squadron in April 1941 (a unit regrouping many of the Canadians serving in the RAF). Quickly, he opened his score on the 13th by damaging a Bf110 then, on 10 May, shot down an He111 during a night patrol followed by another damaged aircraft on 17 August. Two months later, he was posted to No. 611 (West Lancashire) Squadron but moved to No. 340 (Free French) Squadron within three weeks. He became of flight commander in April 1942 and added two confirmed victories (one being shared) before taking command of

No. 174 Squadron flying fighter-bomber Hurricanes in July 1942. He was the first Frenchman to lead a British fighter squadron. He received the DFC on 1 August. During the Dieppe raid (Operation 'Jubilee') of 19 August 1942, while leading his unit during a fighter-bomber mission, his aircraft, HV557, probably collided with a Fw190 which also crashed. This final victory brought his total to four confirmed victories (one being shared) and two damaged aircraft.

Hurricane Mk.IICs of 174 Sqn in May 1942 just before the introduction of the new markings. The squadron was based at Manston at the time. This unit was formed in March 1942 and converted to Typhoons one year later. Despite its mission as fighter-bombers, 174 managed to make about 18 claims on Hurricanes.
(via Andrew Thomas)

GIBBES,
Robert Henry Maxwell, RAAF

AUS. 260714

Australian

DSO, DFC & Bar

'Bobby' Gibbes from New South Wales, Australia, joined the RAAF in February 1940 and served initially with No. 23 Squadron RAAF. He was then posted to No. 450 (RAAF) Squadron, as it was forming, in March 1941 as a Flying Officer. He followed the unit to the Middle East where he switched to **No. 3 Squadron RAAF** as it was converting to Tomahawks for the Syrian campaign. He opened his score on 11 July 1941 by claiming a confirmed French Dewoitine 520. Later in the Western Desert he proved to be a resolute fighter and increased his tally and gained rapid promotion. He took command of the squadron, now flying Kittyhawks, in February 1942. In May he was shot down by return fire from a Ju88 and bailed out but broke his ankle. After one month away from the squadron he returned at the head of his unit with his leg still in plaster. In July he was awarded the DFC. In January 1943 he received an immediate DSO after saving one of his pilots shot down in the desert by landing, picking him up and taking off despite severely damaging part of his undercarriage. He was shot down a second time on 16 January behind enemy lines but was able to evade capture; he made his final claim on 22 January. He continued to lead the squadron until April 1943, close to the end of the Tunisian campaign, and received a Bar to his DFC in May. His tally at the time was twelve confirmed victories, two being shared, four probable and sixteen aircraft damaged. He was repatriated to Australia where he served as flying instructor. In October 1944, he began a second tour of operations as Wing Commander and Wing Leader of **No. 80 Wing RAAF** in the South West Pacific. Flying Spitfires, he left that position in April 1945. He was eventually released from the RAAF in January 1946.

Curtiss Tomahawk IIB AN325/W of 3 Sqn RAAF at the end of summer 1941. The squadron claimed close to 70 confirmed and probable victories on Tomahawks. Nine of Gibbes' claims were made while flying the Tomahawk.

'Bobby' Gibbes in board of his personal Spitfire Mk. VIII A58-602/RG-V while acting as Wing Leader of No. 80 Wing in the Southwest Pacific. The letter 'V' was his lucky letter.

GILLAM,
**Denys Edgar,
RAF**

RAF **No. 37167**

British

DSO & Two Bars, DFC & Bar

Denys Gillam joined the RAF in 1935. Upon his training being completed, he was posted to No. 29 Squadron. When war broke out he was serving with the Meteorological Flight but was soon posted to an operational unit, No. 616 (South Yorkshire) Squadron, flying Spitfires. On 1 June he damaged a Ju88 over Dunkirk to open his score. He then participated to the Battle of Britain and made eight claims in August followed by five more in two days on 1 and 2 September before being shot down but managing to bale out. The same day, the squadron was withdrawn for rest but Gillam was posted as a flight commander to the new No. 312 (Czechoslovak) Squadron to fly Hurricanes. One month later he shared the destruction of a Ju88. It was the unit's first kill. He left 312 in November, having been awarded the DFC that month, to command **No. 306 (Polish) Squadron** a position he would hold until the end of his tour in March 1941. Back on operations in July, he was given command of **No. 615 (County of Surrey) Squadron**. However, on 23 November, he was shot down by flak off Dunkirk but was rescued. His wounds kept him away from combat for a few weeks. In December, however, he was awarded the DSO after receiving a Bar to his DFC during the previous October. In March 1942 he was medically fit again and, as a Wing Commander, became the first WingCo Flying of the **Duxford Wing**'s Typhoon squadrons. He led the Wing until October. Over the next year he held various non-flying positions but returned to operations in December 1943 to form a new Typhoon wing at Tangmere. This unit would become **No. 146 Airfield/Wing** (Wing after 12.05.44) on 31 January 1944. Two weeks previously, he had made his last claim, a damaged Fw190, to bring his total to eight confirmed victories (one being shared), three more probable and six aircraft damaged. He left 146 Airfield in March, and was promoted to Group Captain and took over **No. 20 Wing**, but returned to 146 Wing in July as OC when 20 Wing was disbanded. He was awarded a Bar to his DSO in August followed by a second Bar in January 1945 at the end of his command. He left the RAF in October 1945.

Hawker Typhoon R7698/Z-Z of Wing Commander Gillam in the autumn 1942 while Wing Leader of the Duxford Wing.

**Hawker Typhoon Mk IB MN587, G/C D.E. Gillam,
No. 146 Wing, B.70 Deurne/Antwerp, Belgium, autumn 1944**

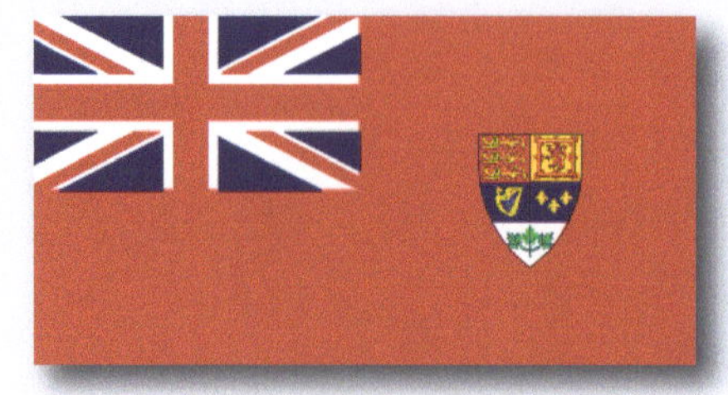

GODEFROY,
**Hugh Constant,
RCAF**

CAN./ J.3701

Canadian

DSO, DFC & Bar

Hugh Godefroy was born in Java, in the Dutch East Indies, to a Dutch father and Canadian mother. However, he was educated in Ontario, Canada and was a student at Toronto University when the war broke out. He volunteered to serve in the RCAF and joined in June 1940. He sailed for the UK in February 1941 and, after a course at No. 56 OTU, was posted to No. 401 (RCAF) Squadron in April to fly Hurricanes and, later, Spitfires. His first tour ended in April 1942 with no claims made. Godefroy returned to 401 in November 1941 and, at last, opened his score on 17 January 1943 by damaging two Fw190s. A confirmed claim against an Fw190 was added three days later. These would be the only claims made while serving with 401 as he was made a move to **No. 403 (RCAF) Squadron** at the end of the month. Claims and promotions followed quickly. He became a flight commander in March and took command of the squadron in June with a DFC received the previous month and left at the of July. In September he was posted to **No. 127 (RCAF) Airfield** as Wing Leader. He made his last claim, an Fw190 destroyed on 24 September, to bring his total to seven aircraft destroyed and three damaged. The same month, he received a Bar to his DFC. He was awarded a DSO in April and ended his tour in May 1944. He was appointed to a staff position in the 2nd TAF and occasionally flew Typhoons until August when he was repatriated to Canada. He left the RCAF in November 1945.

When Godefroy joined No. 401 (RCAF) Squadron in April 1941, the squadron was still equipped with Hurricanes. They would be exchanged for Spitfires in September that year.

**Supermarine Spitfire Mk IX, W/C H.C. Godefroy,
No. 127 Wing, Kenley, United Kingdom, spring 1944**

HAYWARD,
**Robert Kitchener,
RCAF**

CAN./ J.12234

Newfoundlander

DSO, DFC

'Bob' Hayward enlisted in the RCAF in June 1940. Upon completion of his training, he served as an instructor until October 1942 when he was posted overseas. He sailed to the UK, attended an OTU course and was then posted to No. 401 (RCAF) Squadron in March 1943. He remained with 401 until May 1944 during which he made various claims. The first of these was a shared probable Fw190 claimed on 19 July 1943. In May he was posted to

No. 411 (RCAF) Squadron as a flight commander, participating in the invasion of France, and in June he made a double claim over two Fw190s on 28 June. His last claims were made on 4 July and at the end of July his score was six confirmed victories (one shared), one shared probable and six aircraft damaged (one being shared). He took command of the Squadron in August and was awarded the DFC in September. This was followed by a DSO in October (one of the two Newfoundlander airmen to receive such an award). Shortly after he left the squadron tour-expired. He was repatriated to Newfoundland and was released in November 1945.

Spitfire Mk.IX MH850 of 411 Sqn at the time when Hayward arrived at the squadron in the spring of 1944. This unit claimed the destruction of 84 aircraft, 5 more being accepted as probably destroyed. All of these claims were made on Spitfires.

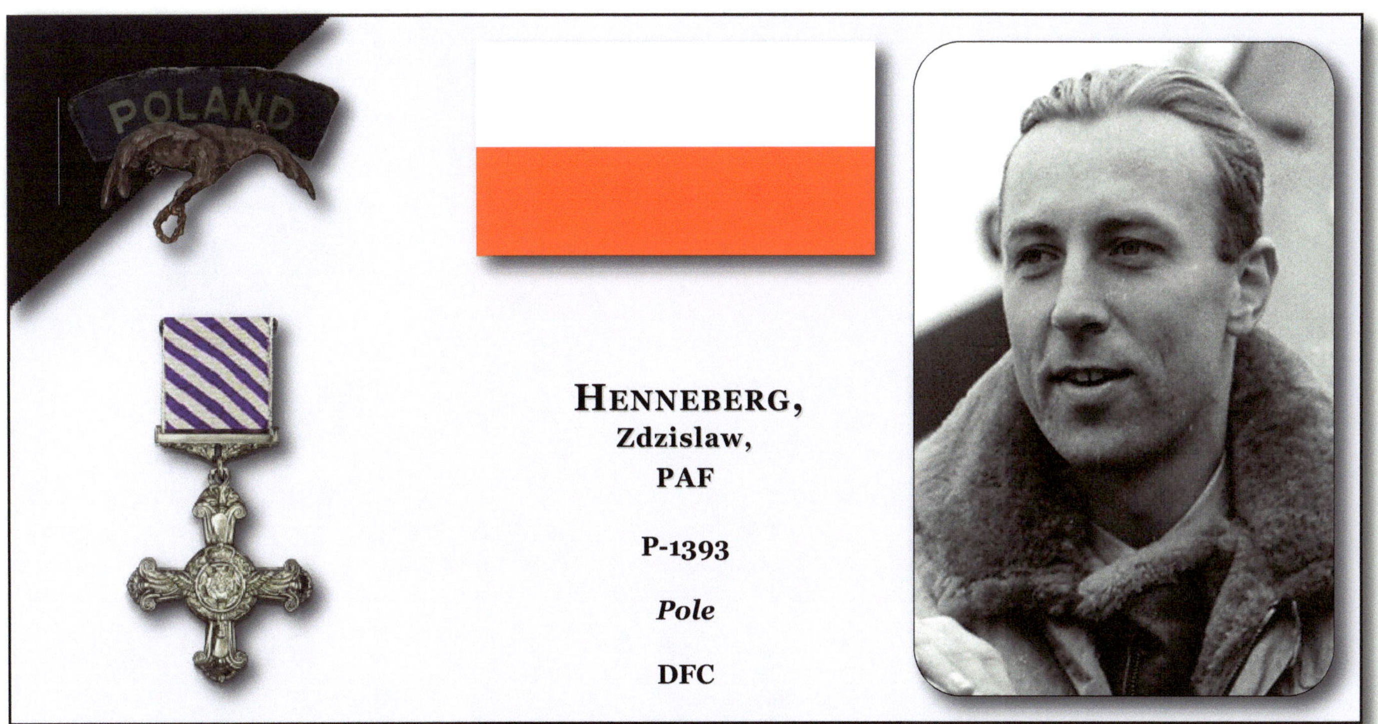

HENNEBERG,
Zdzislaw,
PAF

P-1393

Pole

DFC

Zdzislaw Henneberg was a pre-war flying instructor officer of the Polish Air Force. In September 1939 he fought in a special unit manned by instructors before escaping to France via Romania. There he enlisted in the French Air Force and was appointed to the head of a Defense Flight protecting the Bloch manufacturing plant at Châteauroux. He made his first claim on 5 June by sharing in the destruction of an He111. On 18 June, just after the declaration of the armistice, he led his unit to RAF Tangmere. It was the only Polish unit to fly their aircraft from France to Britain. He was quickly retrained as an RAF fighter pilot and, in August 1940, was posted to **No. 303 (Polish) Squadron**. In the next few weeks he added to his score with eight enemy aircraft destroyed, one probably destroyed and one damaged (the last claim taking place on 5 October). By the end of the month he had become a flight commander too and was awarded the DFC. He took command of the squadron in February 1941 and would lead it until his death on 12 April. He failed to return from a 'Rhubarb' sortie in his Spitfire Mk.II (P8029) after being damaged by flak while attacking a German airfield. He was seen going down in the sea just thirteen miles off Dungeness. He was seen swimming but was never found and is presumed to have drowned.

Hurricane V6665 of 303 (Polish) Sqn during the Battle of Britain. This unit became one of the best Hurricane squadrons of the Battle of Britain with around 140 aircraft claimed as destroyed or probably destroyed. V6665 was lost in combat on 11 September, its Polish pilot dying from his wounds a couple of days later. *(Wilhelm Ratuszynski)*

'Gus' Holden joined the RAF on a short service commission in June 1936. Upon completion of his training in April 1937 he was posted to No. 56 Squadron and remained there until May 1940 when he was posted to **No. 501 (County of Gloucester) Squadron**. This unit went to France a couple of days later. During the Battle of France, he claimed three German bombers as destroyed, the first claim being made on 28 May over a Bf109. With 501, he flew in the Battle of Britain as a flight commander, and added more claims to his tally, but had to be hospitalised which kept him away from operations for seven weeks. Despite this, he was awarded the DFC in August. Returning to his squadron at the end of September in the same position, he made his last claims on 26 October, a Bf109 damaged and his final tally was seven confirmed victories, one shared probable and three damaged aircraft. Two weeks later he took command of the squadron and would lead it until June 1941. This was his last operational posting until the end of war. He continued to serve in the RAF after the war until retirement in December 1964.

Two Hurricane Mk.Is (P3059 and P3208) of 501 Sqn taking off from Hawkinge on 15 August 1940 at the height of the Battle of Britain. The squadron was credited with about 115 enemy aircraft destroyed or probably destroyed during this time. In return, however, the squadron lost over 40 Hurricanes, including these two (both lost on 18 August), on operations.

HORBACZEWSKI,
Eugeniusz,
PAF

P-0273

Pole

DSO, DFC

Eugeniusz Horbaczewski joined the Polish Air Force in 1937. In September 1939 he served in the ferry flight unit and did not participate directly in the air combats against the Germans. He then escaped to France via Romania, and from there was sent to the UK. Re-trained in the RAF as a fighter pilot, his first assignment was No. 303 (Polish) Squadron in August 1941. On 6 November he opened his score by claiming a probable Bf109 and added three confirmed 'kills' while with 303. In September 1942 he was posted to No. 302 (Polish) Squadron where he stayed until the end of his tour in December. Posted as an instructor for a short time, he volunteered for, and was posted to, the Polish Fighting Team destined to go to North Africa with Spitfire Mk.IXs and attached to No. 145 Squadron. He made more claims and was awarded the DFC in July before being posted to No. 601 (County of London) Squadron. A few days later he was posted to **No. 43 Squadron**, initially as a flight commander, but progressed rapidly to become its CO in August. He led the unit for the next two months and achieved further successes before returning to the UK to take command of **No. 315 (Polish) Squadron**, in February 1944, while the unit was converting to the Mustang III. With 315, he participated in the Normandy invasion and had claimed six confirmed victories on Mustangs (one being shared) plus five V-1s (two being shared) by 18 August. On this day he shot down his last three enemy aircraft within fifteen minutes to bring his total to seventeen confirmed victories (one shared), one probable and one damaged aircraft, but was himself shot down and killed (Mustang III FB355). A DSO was awarded several days later.

By the summer of 1942, No. 303 (Polish) Squadron was flying on Spitfire Mk. V. The 303 was the best Polish fighter unit of the war with over 240 confirmed of probable enemy aircraft to its tally.

North American Mustang Mk III FB382, S/L E. Horbaczewski,
No. 315 (Polish) Squadron, Holmsley South and Ford, June-July 1944

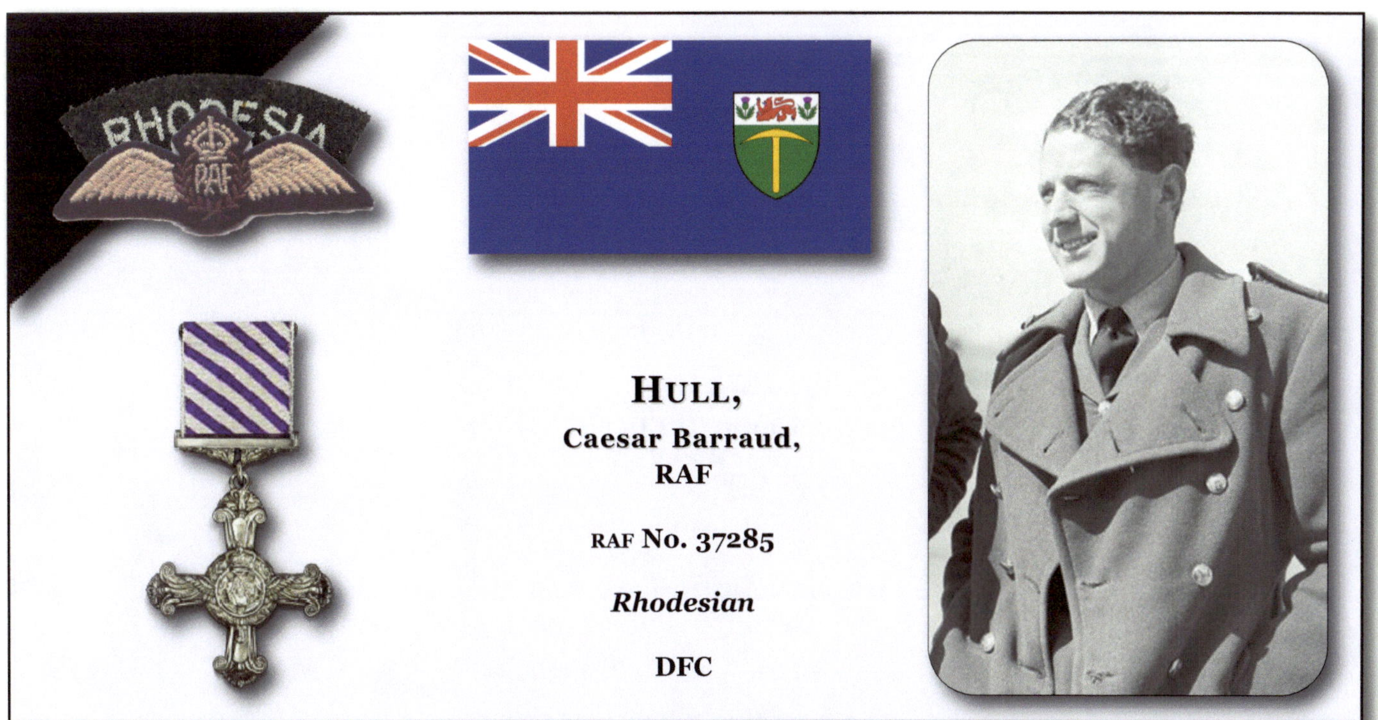

HULL,
Caesar Barraud,
RAF

RAF **No. 37285**

Rhodesian

DFC

Although brought up in South Africa, Hull was born in Southern Rhodesia. His family moved to the Transvaal in South Africa after WW1 and he went to college in Johannesburg. In the mid-thirties Hull applied to join the South African Air Force but was turned down because he could not speak Afrikaans. So he enlisted in the RAF instead in 1935 on a short service commission and, by 1936, he was serving with No. 43 Squadron and flying Hawker Furies. He was still with this squadron, now flying Hurricanes, when war broke out. On 30 January 1940 he shared in the destruction of an He111 (the first victory claimed by the 43) and, during the Phoney War, added two more shared confirmed victories. In May 1940 he was posted to No. 263 Squadron with which he fought in Norway, adding more claims (three confirmed victories and two aircraft damaged), but was shot down and wounded, while making his last claim on the 27th, and was evacuated to the UK three days later. For his actions in Norway he was awarded the DFC. After recovering from his wounds he was posted back to **No. 43 Squadron** at the end of August and promoted to Squadron Leader to replace the previous CO who had been killed in action. Within a week he claimed two probably destroyed Bf110s (on 4 September) and shared in the destruction of a Ju88 two days later. The next day the squadron was scrambled to intercept a large formation of bombers escorted by Bf109s. Hull, flying Hurricane V6641, was shot down and killed by one of the enemy fighters.

A 263 Sqn Gladiator under camouflage made of branches. During the campaign of Norway, and despite the obsolescence of the Gladiator, the pilots of 263 claimed 30 confirmed or probable claims.

JAMES,
Kenneth Elwyn,
RAAF

AUS. 408021

Australian

-

'Skeeter' James, from Victoria, Australia, joined the RAAF in June 1940. He completed his initial training in Australia and, like many other RAAF pilots, ended up in England. On 30 June 1941 he was posted to **No. 457 (RAAF) Squadron** as a Pilot Officer. The squadron was first held in reserve, serving as a kind of post-OTU for its sister unit, No. 452 (RAAF) Squadron, and was not engaged against the Luftwaffe until March 1942. On 28 March he shared in the destruction of an Fw190 and the following month became the commander of B Flight. Just before the squadron was sent to Australia to defend Darwin, James became the OC, a position he would keep until February 1944. During this time his score against the Japanese rose and he claimed two confirmed and one probable aircraft against them. He made his last claim on 17 August 1943 over a Dinnah.Rested, he started a second tour of operations in September 1944 as OC of **No. 85 Squadron RAAF** which was responsible for the air defence of Western Australia with ageing Spitfire Mk.Vs. He left 85 in March 1945 and, two months later, was posted to command **No. 79 Squadron RAAF** with which he saw combat in the South West Pacific theatre during the last weeks of the war. He left 79 in November and was released from the RAAF in February 1946.

Spitfire A58-163 of 85 Sqn RAAF in 1945. The squadron was the only RAAF unit not to fly the Mk.VIII and flew the obsolete Mk.V until the end of war. The first Spitfires were issued at the time James took over command. Admittedly, the squadron was based around Perth, in Western Australia, where the threat of a Japanese incursion had long since faded away.

KELLAS,
Sminagos Ioanis 'John', RHAF

Greek

DFC

Ioannis Kellas, sometimes known as John Kellas, was a pre-war Royal Hellenic Air Force (RHAF) officer and when the Italians invaded Greece in October 1940 he was in charge of 21 Mira (Squadron) flying Polish-made PZL P.24 fighters. On 20 November 1940 he opened his score by downing down a Cant Z.1007. In January 1941 his unit began to fly on Gloster Gladiators handed over by the RAF. Flying the British biplanes he claimed a shared victory against a Fiat BR20 followed, on 9 February, by two more claims over Italians fighters. On 15 April, during the German invasion, Kellas was hit by a Messerschmitt Bf 109 and made an emergency landing. Soon after, he managed to escape to Egypt. The RHAF re-organised in the Middle East as part of the RAF and Kellas served in non-operational duties for over a year before being posted in September 1942 as OC of **No. 335 (Hellenic) Squadron**. The squadron was about to be deployed to the Western Desert and Kellas led it during the Battle of El Alamein. He left the squadron in November and served in the Ferry Command in the following years, ending the war as a Wing Commander. He received the British DFC after the war in 1948 for his actions against the Italians alongside the RAF in Greece.

A line-up of Hurricanes of 335 (Hellenic) Sqn wearing the codes 'FG' which were worn from October 1941 to September 1942. Because of the lack of reserves, the Greeks were not engaged intensively during the war and even when engaged it was only for a short time.
(via Dimitrios Vassilopoulos)

KILIAN,
John Rutherford Clark, RNZAF

NZ1043

New Zealander

-

John Kilian was a pre-war regular officer, having joined the RNZAF in September 1937. By August 1941, when he sailed for the UK, he was a pilot of immense experience having accumulated almost 2,000 hours of flight time. After attending OTU he served briefly with No. 401 (RCAF) Squadron as a supernumerary Flight Lieutenant, before joining No. 485 (NZ) Squadron in January 1942 in the same capacity. He opened his score on 24 April, by destroying a Fw190 during a circus over France. At the end of May, he took up a flight commander's post with No. 222 (Natal) Squadron and, on 19 June, claimed a Fw190 destroyed, damaging another a month later. His stay with Treble Two Squadron was short because, in August, he was promoted to command **No. 122 (Bombay) Squadron**. He participated in Operation '*Jubilee*' over Dieppe sharing in the destruction of a Do217, but was slightly wounded in a follow up operation that same day. He left the squadron during November on rest and, towards the end of March 1943, was given command of **No. 504 (County of Nottingham) Squadron**. He remained with the unit until July, damaging a Fw190 on 4 April, which brought his tally to three confirmed victories, one being shared, and two aircraft damaged. He returned to New Zealand later in the year and, in July 1944, commenced operations flying Corsairs in the South West Pacific, as OC of **No. 19 Squadron, RNZAF**. On 25 December, he parachuted after his aircraft had been hitby ground fire but was rescued uninjured, from the sea, by an American flying boat. In June 1945 he became OC **No. 14 Squadron, RNZAF**, which flew up to Emirau, from where it was operating when the war with Japan ended. Kilian relinquished command of the squadron the following month and was demobbed from the RNZAF in 1946.

A RNZAF Corsair undergoing maintenance in the Solomon's. The RNZAF took delivery of 424 Corsairs during the war to equip 13 fighter squadrons.

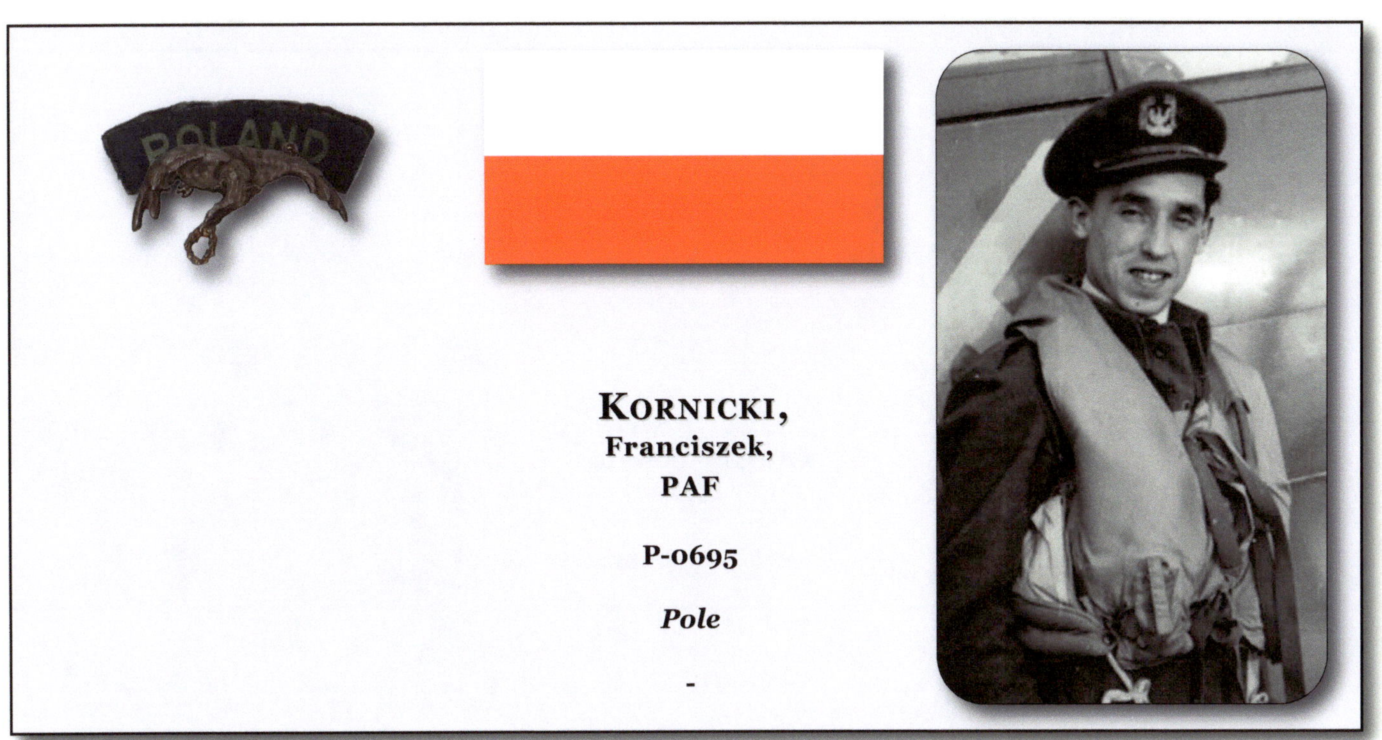

KORNICKI,
Franciszek,
PAF

P-0695

Pole

-

Franciszek Kornicki enlisted in the pre-war Polish Air Force and completed his training as a fighter pilot, just in time to resist the German invasion, but flew obsolete PZL P.7s. In mid-September 1939 he escaped to Romania then continued his travel to France, where he underwent a fighter pilot training and finally to the UK where he was re-trained as an RAF fighter pilot and posted to No. 303 (Polish) Squadron in October 1940 (after a false start at No. 307 (Polish) Squadron, the Polish night fighter unit). In January 1941 he was sent to No. 315 (Polish) Squadron, then under formation, and he remained with that unit until February 1943 when he left to take command of **No. 308 (Polish) Squadron**. He was the youngest Polish squadron commander at that time but had to relinquish command within a fortnight due to health problems. Kornicki returned to operations in May 1943 and took command of **No. 317 (Polish) Squadron** until December. He then served in non-flying positions until the end of war. He stayed in the UK after the war and served with the RAF until 1972.

317 (Polish) Sqn was the last Polish fighter squadron to be formed. It transitioned to the Spitfire Mk.IX in September 1943 but only ten confirmed or probable claims were made by the squadron's pilots while flying this mark. In all, 317 claimed the destruction of 48 enemy aircraft (one being shared) and 11 more as probables.
(Wilhelm Ratuszynski)

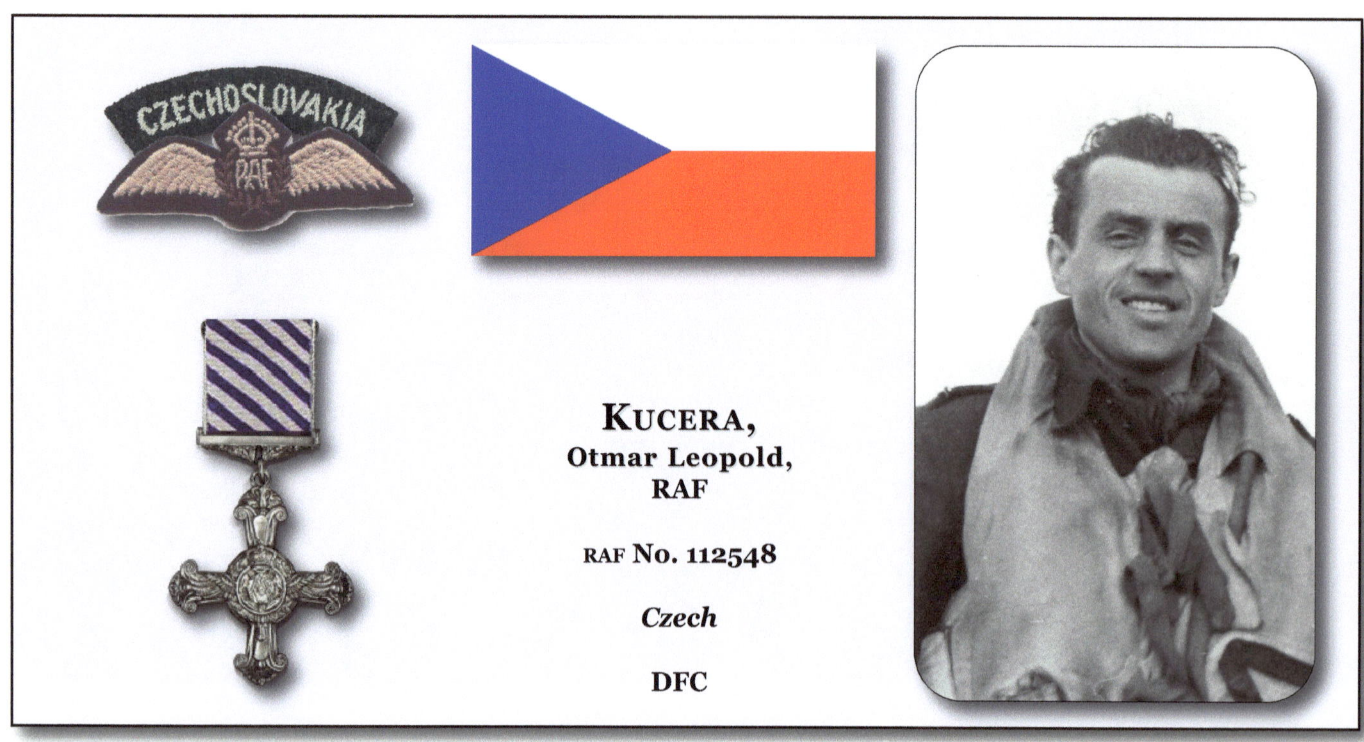

KUCERA,
Otmar Leopold,
RAF

RAF No. 112548

Czech

DFC

Otmar Kučera was a fighter pilot in the Czechoslovakian Air Force when the Germans occupied his country in March 1939. He escaped to France, via Hungary, Yugoslavia and Lebanon, and enlisted in the French Air Force in March 1940. He did not see any action during the Battle of France and escaped once more, but to the UK this time, and enlisted in the RAF in August 1940. Retrained, he was posted to No. 111 Squadron in October 1940 as an NCO. He made his first claim on 13 November, sharing in the destruction of an He111, and another one two days later and added an aircraft damaged in March. He was then posted to No. 312 (Czechoslovakian) Squadron the next month where he claimed three more confirmed victories and one more probable. He received his commission in November and remained with this squadron until April 1942 when he was posted to **No. 313 (Czechoslovakian) Squadron**. In June his tour was completed but he had added a confirmed Fw190 to his credit on 5 May. A DFC was awarded in October. In January 1943 he returned to 313 for a second tour of operations. Becoming a flight commander in September, he claimed his last victory on the 27th to bring his total to seven confirmed victories (two being shared), one probable and one aircraft damaged. His second tour was completed in May 1944 but he returned a third time to 313 in November as its OC and led the unit until the end of war. He served in the post-war Czechoslovakian Air Force but was arrested in January 1949 by the new Communist regime and released after six months of jail. That put an end to his military career.

Spitfire HF.IX ML148 of 313 Sqn photographed during the spring of 1945. This Spitfire was the usually flown by Otmar Kučera and 313 was engaged in escort missions for the bombers of Bomber Command which had returned to daylight raids in 1945. The squadron is credited with 11 confirmed victories and 6 probables during the war. All of these were claimed on Spitfire Mk.Vs.
(Andrew Thomas)

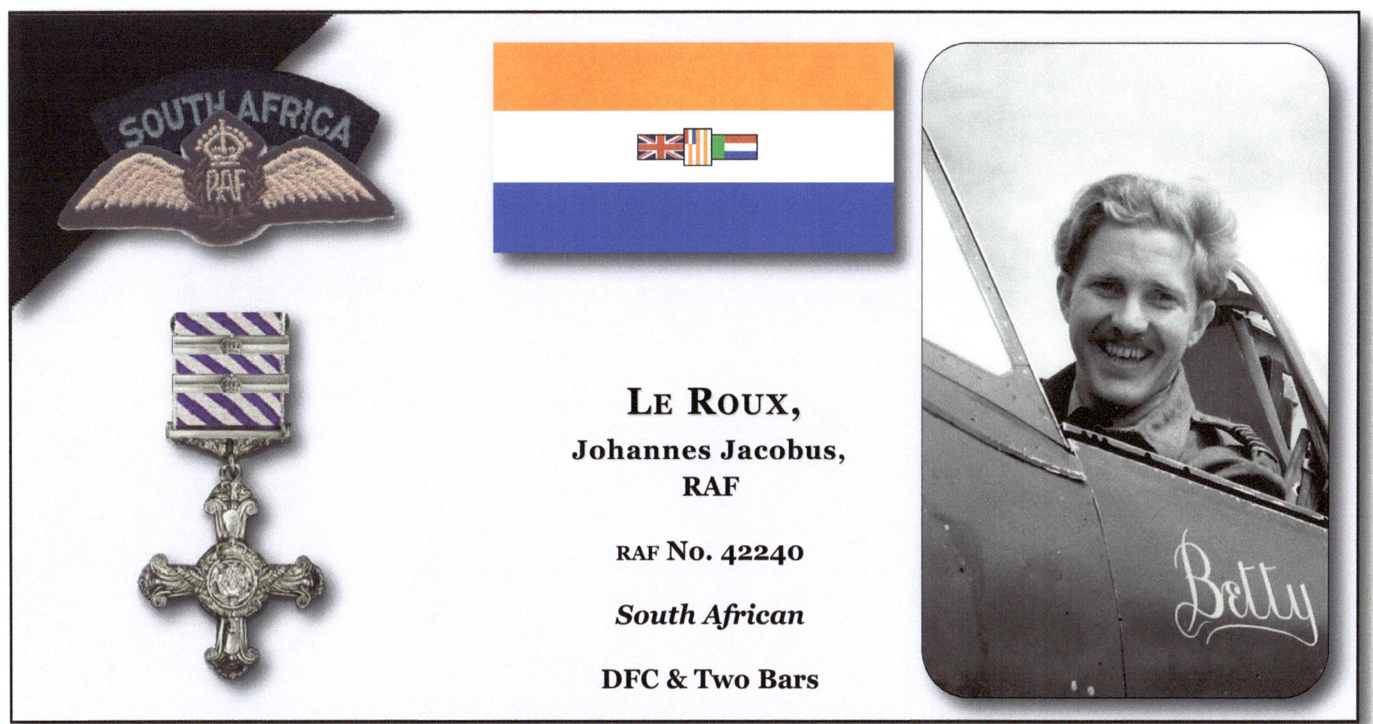

LE ROUX,
Johannes Jacobus, RAF

RAF **No. 42240**

South African

DFC & Two Bars

'Chris' Le Roux, after first attempting to join the SAAF before the war, decided to join the RAF in February 1939 on a short service commission. One year later he was posted to No. 73 Squadron and then to No. 85 Squadron (both based in France and flying Hurricanes) with which he participated in the brief Battle of France. Wounded in action, he was repatriated at the end of May. Upon recovery he initially became an instructor but was then posted to No. 41 Squadron in December 1940 to fly Spitfires. In February he joined No. 91 (Nigeria) Squadron, with which he stayed until the end of his tour in December 1941, and rose to flight commander. During his stay with 91 he claimed six confirmed victories, one probable and two damaged aircraft, and received a DFC in October. He started another tour in September 1942 as supernumerary with No. 91 Squadron and, before leaving for the Middle East in January, he claimed two more confirmed victories and two aircraft damaged, and added a Bar to his DFC in December. In the Middle East he joined **No. 111 Squadron**, flying Spitfires, when he took command of the unit between January and April 1943 during the Tunisian campaign. He recorded more successes with four confirmed, one probable and two damaged. He returned to the UK and a second Bar to his DFC was awarded in July before he became a fighter controller until July 1944 when he was posted to **No. 602 (City of Glasgow) Squadron** as OC. Within two weeks he claimed his last victories to bring his score to eighteen confirmed, two probable and eight damaged. He made his last claim on 31 July over a Fw190. He is thought to have been the pilot that strafed and wounded Erwin Rommel on 17 July. However, on 29 August, Le Roux took off, in Spitfire PL155, to fly to England but never arrived.

A Spitfire of 602 Sqn, during the early stages of the Battle of Normandy, with the full D-Day markings painted on. The squadron claimed 26 aircraft destroyed or probably destroyed between D-Day and the end of August 1944.

MALENGREAU,
Roger Fulgence Fernand Ghislain, RAF

RAF No. 82160

Belgian

-

Roger Malengreau enlisted in the Belgian Army in 1936 to become a pilot. In May 1940 he was an Army Cooperation pilot flying Fairey Foxes when Belgium was invaded by the Germans. Within two days his unit lost all of its aircraft and the personnel escaped to France. Continuing his retreat in France, despite the fact that Belgium had surrendered, Malengreau did not return to his country but sailed to the UK instead after France signed the Armistice at the end of June 1940. Arriving in England on 9 July, he enlisted in the RAF and was re-trained as a fighter pilot and, upon completion of his training, was posted to No. 87 Squadron in August. He was one of the 29 Belgians to participate in the Battle of Britain. In December he was posted to No. 56 Squadron, then to No. 609 Squadron and opened his score on 30 June 1941, sharing the probable destruction of a Bf109 and adding another probable on 14 July. In October 1942 he was posted to No. 171 Squadron but in November he was offered the position of CO of the second Belgian fighter unit, **No. 349 (Belgian) Squadron**, then based in Nigeria in Western Africa. He accepted this posting and officially took over on 1 January 1943. At his own request, the squadron, which was intended to serve in the Belgian Congo, was eventually repatriated to the UK, where it was thought it would be more useful, and he left 349 upon arrival back in England. No more operational postings followed before the end of war and he left the military after the war and began a career in the Belgian Foreign Service.

A very rare photo of a Belgian Tomahawk under maintenance in Nigeria. The formation of 349 Sqn was made at the time when the Germans could take control of North Africa. This would have left the Belgian Congo defenseless.
(André Bar)

MANAK,
Jiri,
RAF

RAF **No. 81896**

Czech

DFC

Jiří Maňák was a former pre-war Czechoslovakian Air Force observer when he decided to flee to France. There, he was re-trained as a fighter pilot but France collapsed before he could join any operational unit. He escaped to the UK and, in August 1940, was posted to No. 310 (Czechoslovakian) Squadron, under formation, as a reserve pilot pending training on Hurricanes which took place in September. In November he was posted to No. 601 (County of London) Squadron where he claimed two confirmed victories in the following spring (6 May and 2 June). Ending his tour in November 1941, he served a flying instructor before starting a new tour in July 1942 with No. 81 Squadron but left this unit to join No. 611 (West Lancashire) Squadron with which he added two aircraft damaged (the last on 5 September) to his tally just before being posted to No. 182 Squadron in September as a flight commander. This unit was to be re-equipped with the Hawker Typhoon and Maňák became one of the very few Czechoslovakian pilots to fly operations on the type. He remained with 182 until being promoted to Squadron Leader and given command of **No. 198 Squadron**, another Typhoon unit, in May 1943. However, on 28 August, flying his 300th sortie, his Typhoon, JP613/TP-N, was hit by flak near Knokke in Belgium and he had to ditch his aircraft into the sea. He managed to get into his dinghy but was picked up by the Germans the next day and spent the rest of the war as a PoW. He was awarded the DFC in January 1944. He served with the post-war Czechoslovakian Air Force but was arrested in 1950 by the new Communist authorities and released in 1951. He was later reinstated and became an airline pilot with CSA.

One the first Typhoons of 182 Sqn, R8991. Maňák achieved the first operational sortie for 182 on 3 January 1943. This Typhoon would be lost the following 13 May when it crash-landed after having been hit by flak.
(D.J.M.Coxhead via C. Thomas)

MANNIX,
Robert Louis,
RAF

RAF No. 64864

American

-

Robert Mannix was an American from New York State. In 1940 he decided to join the Eagle pilots via the Clayton Knight Commitee which was organising the recruitment of these pilots destined to fight in England. He was finally accepted in December 1940. Having about 150 hours of flying time already under his belt, he was sent to an RAF Refresher Training Program in the USA and, in March 1941, crossed the Canadian border where he enlisted in the RAF. He soon sailed to the UK and completed his training at No. 56 OTU before reporting to No. 71 (Eagle) Squadron in June 1941. He claimed one Bf109 as a probable on 2 July (flying a Hurricane) followed by another one on 4 September (this time in a Spitfire) before being sent on leave to the USA in February 1942. He returned to 71 in April but only for a few days as he had volunteered to serve overseas and sailed to the Middle East. He was posted first to No. 127 Squadron in June 1942 as a flight commander, adding one Bf109 damaged and another confirmed destroyed, before being posted out on the last day of October to take command of **No. 33 Squadron**.

His command was short-lived however as he was shot down and killed on 18 November, by a Bf109 of JG27, while undertaking a long-range strafing operation along the road south of Benghazi in Libya.

Hurricane Mk.IIs of 71 Sqn (code XR) in July 1941 while stationed at North Weald. It was the time when 71 made its first claims against the Luftwaffe. Mannix was among the first six pilots to score. The squadron made a dozen claims before converting to the Spitfire in August 1941.

'Gatty' May, from New South Wales, Australia, joined the RAAF in June 1940. He completed his training in Canada in July 1941 and then sailed to the UK where he attended his final course at No. 53 OTU. In October he was posted to No. 66 Squadron as a Pilot Officer and then, in December, to **No. 79 (Madras Presidency) Squadron**. Three months later the squadron left for India and sealed May's fate until the end of war. He participated in every action that 79 was involved in during his first tour. He finished his tour in November 1943 as a Flight Lieutenant. Earlier in the year he had the opportunity to make some claims, the first on 25 March, when he damaged a Ki-43, and another probably destroyed on the 30th. These would be his only claims of the war. In the first days of October 1944, he started a second tour with No. 258 Squadron as a flight commander but was posted to his former squadron, 79, to take command at the end of November. He would lead the squadron over Burma until August 1945, participating in the liberation of Rangoon, and was then repatriated to Australia. He was awarded a DSO the following month and was discharged in December.

Thunderbolt HD247/NV-K of 79 Sqn in 1945. This squadron remains the RAF unit that carried out the highest number of sorties on the Thunderbolt, over 2600, and almost all were completed under the command of 'Gatty' May.

McLeod,
Henry Wallace, RCAF

Can./ J.4912

Canadian

DSO, DFC & Bar

A native of Saskatchewan in Canada, 'Wally' McLeod joined the RCAF in September 1940. He completed his training and reached the UK in April 1941 as a Pilot Officer. After his OTU training, he was posted to No. 132 (Bombay) Squadron to fly Spitfires and was then posted to No. 485 (NZ) Squadron in August where he made his first claim, a Bf 109 damaged, on 27 September. In December he moved to No. 602 (City of Glasgow) Squadron but, almost immediately, moved again to No. 411 (RCAF) Squadron where he made two more claims. In May he was posted overseas and served with both No. 603 (City of Edinburgh) and 1435 Squadrons in Malta. His tally increased rapidly and, at the end of August, he became a flight commander with 1435. In October he received the DFC and the following month he added a Bar. By that time he had left Malta with a tally of thirteen confirmed destroyed aircraft, three more probables and thirteen damaged (one being shared) and had become one of the Malta top scorers. He returned to Canada where he served as a flying instructor at No. 1 OTU at Bagotville (Quebec) until January 1944. He returned to the UK and in February 1944 was given command of the newly-formed **No. 443 (RCAF) Squadron**. He led the squadron during the invasion of Normandy where the squadron met with considerable success and he claimed eight more aircraft as destroyed, the last on 30 July, to bring his total for confirmed 'kills' to twenty-one. He was the RCAF top-scorer of the war at the time. A logical DSO was therefore awarded to McLeod early in September 1944 but, two weeks later, while leading the squadron during the Arnhem operations on 27 September, three years after his first claim, he was engaged by Bf109s and shot down and killed in his Spitfire Mk.IX (NH245).

Spitfires of 443 (RCAF) Sqn were among the first Spitfires to land on French soil during Operation 'Overlord'. Clearly identified is MH370/2I-N. Under the leadership of McLeod, the squadron claimed 29 aircraft destroyed or probably destroyed. Eight of these added to McLeod's tally.
(*via Chris Thomas*)

MEHRE,
Helge Olrik,
RNAF

N. 1152

Norwegian

DSO, DFC

Helge Mehre was a regular Norwegian Army aviation officer when the Germans invaded Norway in April 1940. He was a flying instructor at that time. He managed to flee the country and arrived in Canada near Toronto where 'Little Norway', a Norwegian aviation training facility, was located. In the spring of 1941, his training was completed and he sailed to the UK. He was first posted to No. 242 (Canadian) Squadron in June where he made his first claim, a damaged Bf109, on the 21st. In July he added one confirmed Bf109 and another damaged before moving to **No. 331 (Norwegian) Squadron**. He eventually took command of the squadron in January 1942 and stayed in this role until September when his tour expired. He left with a DFC and one more Bf109 destroyed and four more as damaged. In April 1943 he returned to operations, once more as OC of 331, but the next month he was appointed to lead the **North Weald Wing** where he claimed his last victories to bring his total to six confirmed victories and ten aircraft as damaged. In October 1943 he was awarded the DSO. Then, in November, he became OC of **No. 132 Airfield (132 Wing** after 12 May 1944). He left his position in July but no further operational appointments followed before the end of the war. Mehre continued to serve the RNoAF after the war and had reached the rank of Major General by retirement.

When Mehre took over in January 1942, 331 Sqn was equipped with Spitfire Mk.IIs. The squadron used the Spitfire Mk.II for a short time, between November 1941 and April 1942, during which 500 sorties were carried out. No claims were made on the Mk.II however.

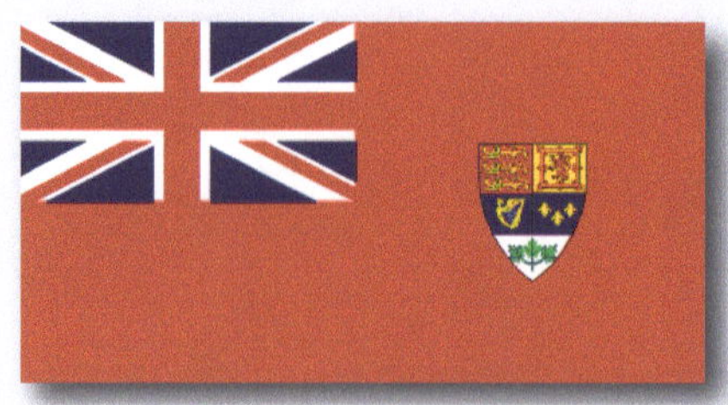

MOLSON,
Hartland de Montarville, RCAF

CAN./ C.1226

Canadian

-

Hartland de Montarville Molson, whose family owned Canada's largest brewery, was born in Montreal, Canada. He served in the Canadian Militia from 1928 to 1933 in the Artillery. Molson joined the RCAF in September 1939 as a regular air force officer and, upon receiving his wings in April 1940, and completion of advanced training, proceeded overseas with No.1 Fighter Squadron RCAF with which he served during the Battle of Britain flying Hurricanes. He managed to damage a Do17 on 26 August, two Bf110s on 4 September, and destroyed a He111 on the 11th. He was shot down and wounded on 5 October and, upon recovery, was repatriated to Canada early in 1941 and posted to **No. 118 Squadron RCAF** recently reformed on the Grumman Goblin. He would eventually command the unit between July 1941 and June 1942 thereafter becoming OC of **No. 126 Squadron RCAF**, flying Hurricanes, before leaving the squadron in September. No more operational postings followed before the end of war. Molson retired from the RCAF as a Group Captain in September 1945 and returned to the family business.

The RCAF was the only operator of the Grumman Goblin. It was introduced into the RCAF inventory because the Canadians were urgently looking for fighters when the country entered the war. The career of this fighter was plagued by many technical problems and eventually the aircraft was withdrawn from use in April 1942 with a poor service record.

Born in England, 'Zulu' Morris was educated in South Africa after his parents had moved there. This, of course, explained the nickname he received in the RAF. He was commissioned in the RAF in 1930 and started his career with No. 40 Squadron flying Fairey Gordons. After a short period with the Fleet Air Arm, he then served as an instructor until 1940 before a posting to the RAF Staff College and a spell at the Air Ministry. In 1941 he served for a short time with the Fighter Interception Unit (FIU) before, in May 1941, being posted as OC of **No. 406 (RCAF) Squadron**, a night fighter squadron under formation, where he would remain until August 1942. Flying with Sergeant A.V. Rix as his radar operator, he claimed three confirmed victories and one aircraft damaged before the end of the year. The first success was achieved on the night of 30 September/1 October against a Ju88. For this action he was awarded a DFC on 21 October. In 1942 he added a final victory in July before relinquishing command the following month. His final tally was four confirmed victories and one damaged aircraft. Various staff positions followed and he took command of **No. 132 (Norwegian) Wing** in November 1944, a position he held until February 1945 when he was promoted to Air Commodore. He was awarded the DSO in May 1945. Morris continued his career after the war and retired as an Air Marshal, and as AOC-in-C Fighter Command, in 1966.

No. 406 Sqn (code HU) was equipped with Beaufighter Mk.IIs between June 1941 and August 1942. The squadron is credited with 59.5 German aircraft destroyed or probably destroyed, including 8 on Beaufighter Mk.IIs.

MORRISON,
Robert Lionel,
SAAF

SAAF No. P203184V

South African

DFC

'Bob' Morrison joined the South African Permanent Force in April 1939. He first served in South Africa before joining **No. 5 Squadron SAAF** in the Western Desert in November 1941 to fly Tomahawks. He opened his score on 12 March when he shared a damaged aircraft. On 27 May he claimed an Italian BR20 bomber as destroyed followed by a second on 3 June which was the same day he was wounded in combat. Returning to his unit in October, he eventually left in March 1943 at the end of his tour as a flight commander and after having added a probable Bf109 on 8 March (his last claim).

In April 1944 he was posted once more to the squadron, now based in Italy, this time as OC. On 13 September his Kittyhawk Mk.IV (FX772) failed to pull out of a bombing dive and he was killed in the crash. He was awarded the DFC in February 1946.

Despite its shortcomings and being out-classed by 1942, the Tomahawk still equipped about half a dozen fighter squadrons in 1941-1942 including three SAAF squadrons. One of these was No. 5 Sqn (codes 'GL'). This unit was credited with 69 victories during the war (over 63 in the Western Desert). *(Michael Schoeman)*

NEIL,
Thomas Francis, RAF

RAF No. 79168

British

DFC & Bar

'Ginger' Neil joined the RAF in October 1938. He completed his course in December 1939 and served at 8 FTS for a couple of weeks before being posted to No. 249 (Gold Coast) Squadron in May 1940 with a commission. Flying Hurricanes, he participated in the Battle of Britain and opened his score on 7 September by shooting down a Bf109. Fourteen other claims followed before the end of October and he was awarded the DFC that month and a Bar the following month. He continued to increase his score and became a flight commander in December. He followed the squadron to Malta in May 1941 and there, on 12 June, he made a final claim over a Bf109 to bring his total to sixteen confirmed victories (four being shared), two probables and one aircraft damaged. He left Malta in December and returned to the UK. After a period of rest as a flying instructor at No. 56 OTU, he started a new tour of operations as OC **No. 41 Squadron** in September 1942. At first flying Merlin-engined Spitfires, 41 became the first to convert to Griffon-engined Spitfires when the new Mk.XII arrived in February 1943. He eventually relinquished command in July 1943. He spent the rest of the war in non-operational positions and retired from the RAF in 1964.

Spitfire Mk.XII MB882/MB-B in flight over the British countryside. The Mk.XII was the first variant of the Spitfire equipped with the Griffon engine to become operational. Only two squadrons were eventually equipped with the type. The squadron claimed 17 aircraft destroyed or probably destroyed (not counting at least 53 V-1s).

NICOLSON,
James Brindley Eric, RAF

RAF **No. 39329**

British

VC, DFC

Eric Nicolson joined the RAF in 1936 on a short service commission. In August 1937 he was posted to No. 72 Squadron, with which he started the war, and was then posted to No. 249 Squadron on its formation in May 1940 as a flight commander flying Hurricanes. On 16 August he was surprised by Bf109s and shot down over Southampton. Wounded in the left foot and with a perplex splinter through his left eyelid, Nicolson prepared to abandon his burning Hurricane (P3576). As he did so a Bf110 appeared in front of him. Nicolson slid back into his seat and fired at the enemy fighter. His cockpit was now totally in flames, and he was being burned, but he continued firing until it became impossible to remain and he bailed out. The Bf110 was therefore claimed as probable. He landed safely on the ground but with severe wounds and burns. For his valorous action he was awarded the VC on 15 November and would be the only Fighter Command pilot to receive this decoration. Regaining operational status in September 1941, he was given command of

No. 1459 Flight, a Turbinlite Havoc night fighter unit. In March 1942 he was posted to the Far East in a HQ position with No. 293 Wing. However, he continued to plead for a more active post and was eventually given command of

No. 27 Squadron in August 1943, flying Beaufighters in the fighter-bomber role, and helped to introduce the de Havilland Mosquito into the theatre. He left the squadron in August 1944 and a DFC was awarded the same month. He was posted to various HQ roles in the Far East and in April 1945 was at RAF Burma HQ but still looking for operational flying duties as the war's end approached. On 2 May he managed to fly as a passenger in a Liberator (KH210) of No. 355 Squadron on a bombing sortie but, during the flight to the target, one engine erupted in flames and the Liberator eventually crashed into the sea. Nicolson was among the victims who did not make it out of the aircraft before it sank.

No. 27 Sqn was charged to introduce the Mosquito in the Far East (the Mk.II from April 1943 and the Mk. VI in December the same year). The experiment was terminated in March 1944.

NORSWORTHY,
Hugh Hoyles,
RCAF

CAN./ J.5114

Canadian

DFC

Hugh Norsworthy, from Montreal, Quebec, enlisted in the RCAF in August 1940. He was trained on twin-engine aircraft in Canada and, upon his training being completed, he sailed to the UK in May 1941. He went to No. 54 OTU to become a night fighter pilot and was then posted to No. 85 Squadron in September 1941 to fly the Douglas Havoc. He made his first claim, a Do217 destroyed and shared with a Royal Navy pilot, on the night of 17/18 January 1942. During the year, he converted to the Mosquito. At the end of January 1943 he was posted to No. 3 Squadron to fly Hawker Typhoons. His stay was short as in March he was sent to the Fighter Interception Unit (FIU) and did not return to the squadron until August. He left again in October and was repatriated to Canada in November. He was sent overseas again in February 1944 and, on arrival in the UK, was posted the following month to command

No. 439 (RCAF) Squadron, again flying Typhoons, as part of 2 TAF. He would lead this unit through the Battle of Normandy until the end of his tour in September 1944. He was repatriated, having received the DFC in September, and released from the RCAF in February 1945.

No. 439 Sqn carried out close to 4000 sorties on Typhoons during which its pilots claimed 11 aircraft destroyed or probably destroyed. However the cost was also high as 41 Typhoons were lost on operations. MN553 was one of them as it was lost to flak on 12 August 1944.
(via Larry Milberry)

PETERSON,
Chesley Gordon,
RAF

RAF **No. 83706**

American

DSO, DFC

'Pete' Peterson was an American from Idaho. Eager to fight in Europe, he sailed to the UK during the summer of 1940, in the middle of the Battle of Britain, where he joined the RAF in August. The USAAC training he had already received helped him to speed up his training and he was soon posted to the newly-formed **No. 71 (Eagle) Squadron** in November. The squadron was the first fighter unit to group the pilots coming from the USA together. In May 1941 he became a flight commander and on 6 July he opened his score by claiming a probable Bf109. It was his only claim on the Hurricane as the squadron converted to the Spitfire soon after. In the following weeks his tally increased, opening the way to a DFC awarded in October, and in November he was called to lead the squadron. He held this position until 71 was transferred to the USAAF as the 334th FS in September 1942. Just before his transfer he was awarded the DSO and became the only 'Eagle' pilot to be honoured with this decoration. At the date of his transfer to the USAAF he had claimed six confirmed enemy aircraft destroyed, three more probables and six damaged. He continued the war by leading the 4th FG, the regrouping of the former 'Eagle' squadrons, and adding two more confirmed victories to his credit. He survived the war and continued his career in the USAF before retiring as a Major General in 1965.

Spitfire Mk.II P7308 of 71 Sqn in August 1941 at the time Peterson was a flight commander. The squadron used the Mk.II for a short time as the Mk.V arrived on strength in September 1941.

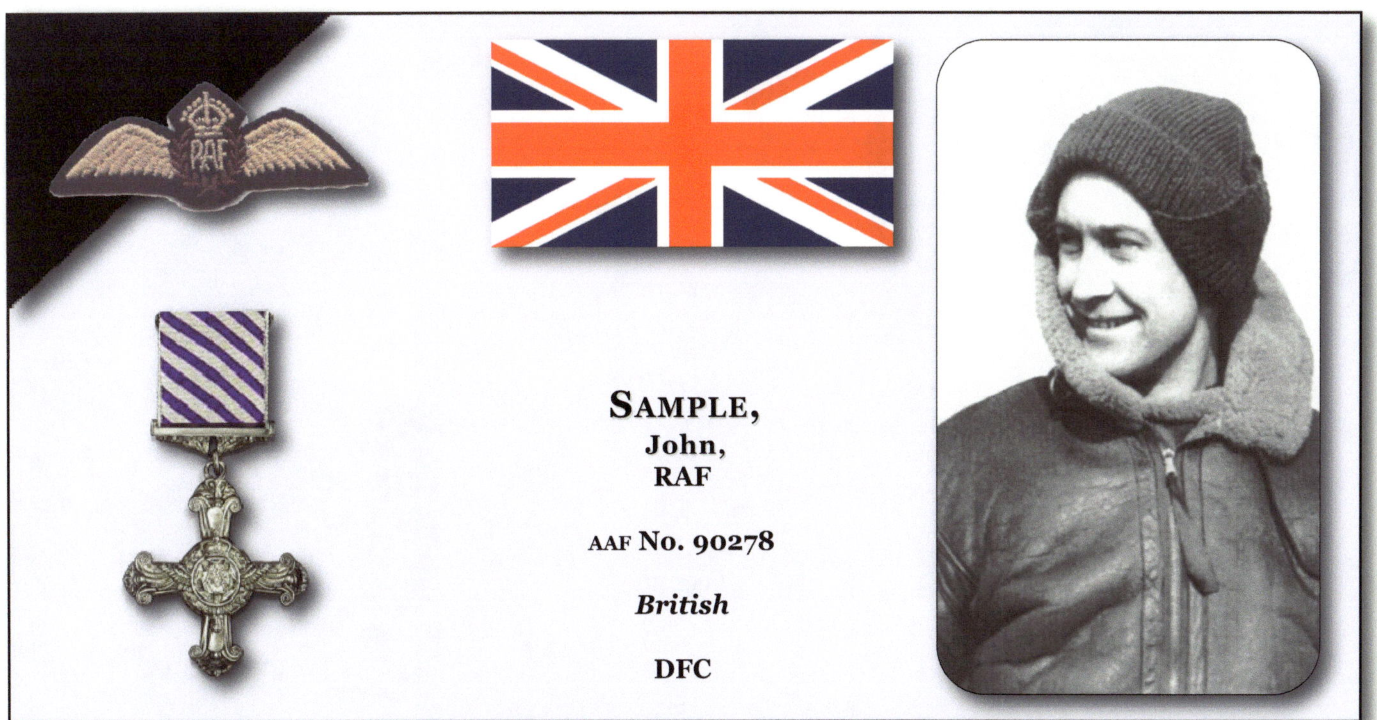

SAMPLE,
John,
RAF

AAF **No. 90278**

British

DFC

'Johnny' Sample joined the Auxiliary Air Force in 1934 as a member of No. 607 (County of Durham) Squadron. By 1939 he was a flight commander and, with war approaching, was called up on 24 August. Still flying Gloster Gladiators, he took part in the only successful interception of an enemy aircraft to be made by UK-based Gladiators and shared in the destruction of a Do18 on 17 October. He moved to France with the squadron in November 1939 and participated in the Battle of France (now flying Hurricanes). On 10 May 1940 he was engaged in combat and made further claims (one shared probable -and two damaged aircraft) but was shot down, slightly injured and repatriated. Before the end of the month he had recovered and was given command of **No. 504 (County of Nottingham) Squadron**. He received the DFC in June. He flew in the Battle of Britain at the head of 504 and added more victories to bring his total to three confirmed (two shared), one shared probable victory, and two aircraft damaged. All of his claims made during the Battle of Britain were made on 15 September.

In March 1941 he was posted for a rest and in September 1941 he was given command of **No. 137 Squadron** as it was forming. The squadron was the second and last unit equipped with the Westland Whirlwind. However, on 28 October 1941, during a practice flight Sample's aircraft (P7053) collided with another Whirlwind of the squadron and he was killed when his parachute failed to open completely.

Whirlwinds of 137 Sqn lined up along the perimeter track at Matlaske early in 1942 with P6982/SF-P in the foreground. The squadron soldiered on with the Whirlwind until June 1943 and completed close to 2250 sorties on the type.
(Chris Thomas)

SCHLOESING,
Jacques Henri,
FFAF

F. 30438

French

-

When the war broke out in 1939 Jacques Schloesing was called up for military duty. He asked to serve in the air force. He was still under training as an observer when France collapsed in 1940.

Dedicated to continuing the struggle, he managed to escape on 22 June 1940 before the armistice. Upon his arrival in the UK he enlisted in the FFAF and requested fighter pilot training. He was posted to No. 17 Squadron in October 1941, then No. 132 Squadron, and then to the newly- formed **No. 340 (Free French) Squadron** the following month. In autumn 1942 he became a flight commander and opened his score on 2 November 1942 by sharing a probable Fw190 over France. He then became the OC in December. However, on 13 February 1943, he was shot down in flames by Fw190s and bailed out, severely wounded, having sustained severe burns. Despite his wounds, he managed to evade capture and was able to return to the UK in June. He recovered and in April 1944 he began to re-train as a fighter pilot and two months later was posted again to 340 as supernumerary Squadron Leader. On 24 August he took command of **No. 341 (Free French) Squadron**, based in France, but on 26 August, on his second mission of the day, the formation he was leading was caught by Fw190s and he was shot down and killed in his Spitfire Mk.IX (PL395).

When Schloesing arrived at 340 Sqn (code GW) in November 1941, the unit was working up on ageing Spitfire Mk.IIs before beco-ming trully operational on Mk.Vs.

SEATON,
Dunham Hodgson,
RAF

RAF **No. 46705**

British

DFC

'Tom' Seaton was a pre-war regular Army officer, commissioned in the *Wiltshire Regiment (Duke of Edinburgh's)*, and joined the Commandos when they were initially formed and saw action with them. However, in August 1941, he joined the RAF and was trained in Canada. Upon completion of his training he was posted to No. 501 (County of Gloucester) Squadron in September 1942. One year later he became a flight commander and finished his first tour in May 1944. In January 1945 he was posted as OC of **No. 611 (West Lancashire) Squadron**, first flying Spitfires and, from March 1945, Mustang Mk.IVs. He led the squadron until the end of war and received a DFC in August 1945. Seaton continued to serve in the RAF and retired as a Group Captain in May 1964.

Mustang Mk.IV KH746 of 611 Sqn which converted to this type in March 1945. In about 220 sorties, the squadron claimed 7 German aircraft destroyed or probably destroyed.
(via Andrew Thomas)

van Lierde,
Rémy,
RAF

RAF No. 106250

Belgian

DFC & Two Bars

'Mony' van Lierde joined the Belgian Air Corps in 1935. By May 1940 he had become an experienced NCO pilot with 1,000 hours flying the Fairey Fox in an Army Co-operation role. He participated in the attempt to stop the German offensive but was injured in combat on 16 May and taken prisoner at the hospital on 29 May. The next day he had recovered enough to escape and in September made the decision to travel to the UK via Gibraltar. Interned in Spain for a short time he did manage to reach Gibraltar and sailed for the UK in July 1941.

Enlisting in the RAF upon his arrival, he was re-trained as a fighter pilot and posted to No. 609 Squadron in January 1942 where the Belgians had formed a Flight. He opened his score soon after by damaging a Do217 on 6 February. Transitioning from the Spitfire to the Typhoon in April 1942, his score increased, over eighteen months, to six confirmed victories until his tour ended in December 1943. A DFC had been awarded the previous June.

In April 1944 he started another tour, posted as a flight commander to No. 3 Squadron, flying Tempests, where he distinguished himself in the V-1 hunt by destroying 37 of the flying bombs (six being shared) during the summer. A Bar to his DFC was approved in July. In August he was posted as OC of **No. 164 (Argentine-British) Squadron**, returning to Typhoons, and held this position until January 1945 when his tour ended. He then fulfilled several HQ postings to 2 TAF. For his leadership and actions with 164 van Lierde was awarded a second Bar to his DFC and became the only Belgian pilot to have receive this decoration three times. He continued his career with the newly-formed Belgian Air Force after the war and retired as a Brigadier General in January 1968.

During the summer 1944 'Mony' van Lierde made most of his claims against V-1s flying this Tempest Mk. V, JN862/JF-Z. No. 3 Sqn remains the best V-1 hunting Tempest unit with around 315 of the flying bombs destroyed.

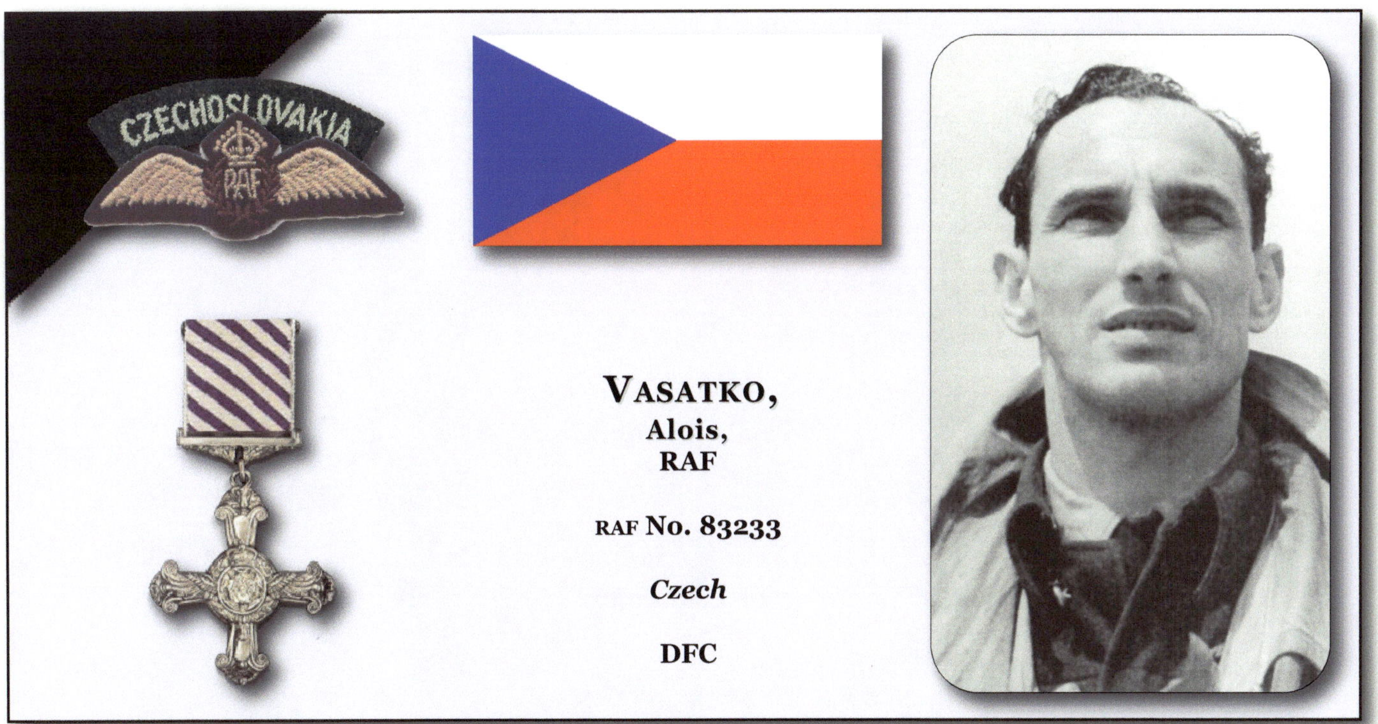

VASATKO,
Alois,
RAF

RAF **No. 83233**

Czech

DFC

Alois Vašátko served with the Czechoslovakian Air Force before the war as a pilot in a two-seat observation aircraft unit. When the Germans occupied his country, he escaped to Poland in July 1939 and then reached France where he enlisted in the French Air Force at the outbreak of war. He was retrained as a fighter pilot and in May 1940 he was serving with a Curtiss fighter unit (CG I/5) when the invasion took place. He claimed his first success against a Bf109 on 17 May and when the Battle of France ended his tally had arisen to twelve confirmed victories (with all but two being shared) and two probables. He flew to Algeria in June 1940 and from there he set out to make his way to England via Morocco and Gibraltar. Upon arrival in England he joined the RAF in August 1940 and in September, was posted to **No. 312 (Czechoslovakian) Squadron** as a founder member flying Hurricanes. One month later, on 8 October, he shared in the destruction of a Ju88, the squadron's first victory. His experience led him to become a flight commander in April 1941, and then the OC in June, as he continued to add more claims to his tally. In May 1942 he left 312 to become the Wing Leader of the **Exeter Wing** which eventually grouped together the three Czech fighter squadrons of the RAF. He was, therefore, the first CO of the 'Czechoslovak Wing' and became the first Czech to command such a formation in the RAF. Sadly his command did not last long as, on 23 June 1942, while flying Spitfire BM592/AV, he collided with an Fw190 during a dogfight while leading the Czech Wing near Île de Batz in France. A DFC was gazetted the following month. With the RAF Vašátko claimed two confirmed victories (one shared), two probables and one damaged aircraft.

As one of many newly-formed fighter units in 1940, 312 was first equipped with Hurricane Mk.Is. These were replaced by the more powerful Mk.II in May 1941. This Hurricane Mk.I, V7066, was lost in action while attacking a German bomber on 10 April 1940. In all 312 flew close to 1200 sorties with the Hurricane Mk.I during which two confirmed victories were made, including one by Vašátko.
(Jiri Rajlich)

WATTS,
Ronald Graham, RNZAF

NZ404974

New Zealander

-

'Ron' Watts joined the RNZAF in December 1940, undertaking preliminary training in New Zealand In March 1941 he sailed for Canada where he completed his Service Flight Training, after which he became a flying instructor at Ternhill in England. In 1943, he attended a night fighter course at OTU and was posted to **No. 488 (NZ) Squadron** in July, flying Mosquito XIIs. Two months later, just before midnight on 15 September, crewed with English navigator Flying Officer Roger Folley, he shot down a Do217. This was the second night victory for the New Zealand squadron, the first having been shot down less than an hour earlier by another crew. In November 1943 he became a flight commander and, in October 1944 assumed command of the Squadron. His second and last victory came on the night of 23 December 1944, when he and his Kiwi navigator, Flying Officer Irwin Skudder, destroyed a Ju188, flying a Mosqutio XXX. Watts continued to lead the squadron until it was disbanded in April 1945. He returned to New Zealand and was released from the RNZAF in March 1946.

A 488 Squadron Mosquito Mk. XIII ME-Z on a night flying test from Amiens-Glisy B48 in France during the summer of 1944. 488 Squadron is credited with 67 confirmed and 3 probable victories, all while operating Mosquitoes on night operations.
(R.G. Watts via P. Sortehaug)

WELLS,
Edward Preston, RNZAF

NZ39950

New Zealander

DSO, DFC & Bar

'Hawkeye' Wells joined the RNZAF in October 1939. Upon completion of training, he was posted to No. 266 Squadron in August 1940, then to No. 41 Squadron in October. With No.41 Squadron he shot down three Bf109s and was also involved in repelling the Italian raid targeting British shipping on 11th November 1940, during which he engaged and damaged a Fiat CR42. He became a founder member of **No. 485 (NZ) Squadron** in March 1941 and rapidly rose through the ranks, becoming a flight commander and, in November, it's Commanding Officer. During his service with the New Zealand Spitfire Squadron he was credited with eight confirmed victories, twice achieving a double on a single operation, once on the 5th July and again on 21st September 1941. For his successes with Nos. 41 and 485 Squadrons he received the DFC in August 1941, and a Bar in November. During May 1942 he was appointed Wing Leader of the **Kenley Wing**, being rested three months later. He was awarded the DSO in August, becoming the first New Zealander to hold the DSO, DFC & Bar.

He returned to operations in 1943 and became the Wing Leader again of Kenley, between August and November, after which he was posted to HQ 11 Group. In March 1944 he flew as supernumerary Wing Commander with No. 144 Wing, adding a last claim on 28 March. This brought his total to twelve enemy aircraft confirmed, four probable, and seven damaged, one of which was shared. In mid-May he became Wing Co flying of **Detling Wing**, the **West Malling Wing** in July, and finally the **Hawkinge Wing** in August. At the beginning of November he became tour expired. Wells was released from the RNZAF in 1947 to take a permanent commission in the RAF, retiring as a Group Captain in 1960.

Spitfire Mk. Vs of No. 485 Sqn seen here at Redhill during the summer of 1941. Some of the squadron's early Spitfire Mk.Vs were funded by New Zealand and it's Pacific Island protectorates. In the forefront is one such machine- AB918/OU-Y 'Wellington I'.*(via P. Sortehaug)*

When war broke out in September 1939, 'Pop' Wheeler was about to turn 41. Wheeler fought to the First World War as an officer of the *Rifle Brigade* and later on, in the North Russia intervention with his new corps, the *Royal Fusiliers*, where he was awarded the Military Cross and Bar in a couple of days. He returned to civilian life in 1920 and occupied various jobs but, by September 1939, had become a commercial pilot and was flying for an airline in Egypt. He enlisted in the RAF in January 1940 and lied about his age so it was not thought he was too old for an operational posting. In July 1940 he was posted to No. 500 Squadron, flying Ansons for Coastal Command, and in November 1940 was transferred to Fighter Command's No. 85 Squadron to fly Hurricanes, Douglas Havocs and Bristol Beaufighters. He made two claims during his time with the squadron - a probable He111 on 6 May and a Ju88 damaged two nights later. In September 1941 he was awarded the DFC. Three months later he was posted to a Beaufighter unit, **No. 219 Squadron**, as OC, and held this position until the end of his tour in June 1942. In December 1942 he returned to operations and took command of **No. 157 Squadron**. Flying the Mosquito, he led the first offensive intruder operation by the squadron on 23 March 1943. He did not make any more claims before being posted out in August 1943. The following month he received a Bar to his DFC. Wheeler decided to convert to heavy bombers soon after and, after re-training, was posted to No. 207 Squadron, a Lancaster unit, in February 1944. He flew a couple of missions over Germany before being shot down by flak with his crew over Frankfurt in the early hours of 23 March 1944.

Mosquito NF.II W4092 of 157 Sqn. This unit is credited with 57 enemy aircraft destroyed or probably destroyed while flying the Mosquito.

WIGHTMAN,
William Taylor Forest, RAF

RAF No. 26129

British

DFC

Wightman was a regular RAF officer and had reached the rank of Squadron Leader by August 1938. In March 1939 he was given command of **No. 94 Squadron** on re-formation at Aden. When Italy declared war against the British Empire in June 1940, the squadron and its Gladiators were involved in various defensive patrols over Aden and British Somaliland. On 2 July Wightman opened his score by shooting down a Fiat CR.42 and on 15 September he damaged a S.79. By May 1941 he had made further claims to bring his total to three confirmed victories and one damaged. The last claim was made on 29 over a Fiat CR.42. A DFC was received in February 1941.

He then moved with the squadron to Iraq in May and converted to the Hurricane at the same time. He left the squadron in July and was posted to non-operational duties for the rest of the war.

He continued to serve in the RAF after the war before retiring in 1958.

Camouflaged and wearing unit code letters and toned down roundels, Gladiator Mk.II N2288/GO-A is seen at Sheikh Othman (Aden) in 1940. This aircraft was involved in the first successful defense of Aden, on the night of 13 June, against the Italian bombers. While under Wightman's command and flying Gladiators, the squadron claimed ten Italian aircraft destroyed or probably destroyed.
(I. Simpson via Andrew Thomas)

SQUADRONS!
No.3
Fighter Leaders
of the RAF, RAAF, RCAF, RNZAF & SAAF in WW2
Volume I
Phil H. Listemann
Fighter Leaders
of the RAF, RAAF, RCAF, RNZAF & SAAF in WW2
Volume III
Phil H. Listemann
USN AIRCRAFT 1922-1962
G-228
Vol.4:
Type Designation Letters
'BF', 'BT' & 'F' (Pt-1)
RAF, Dominion & Allied Squadrons
at War:
Study, History and Statistics
No.137 Squadron
1941 - 1945
COMPILED BY
PHIL H. LISTEMANN
WITH
CHRIS THOMAS
SQUADRONS!
No.10
The North American
Mustang Mk. IV
in Western Europe
www.RAF-IN-COMBAT.com
- USN Aircraft 1922-1962 -
- Squadrons! -
- RAF, Dominion and Allied squadrons at War -
- Allied Wings -
- Famous squadrons of WW2 -
- Fighter Leaders -
RAF, Dominion & Allied Squadron
at War:
Study, History and Statistics
No.131 (County of Kent) Squadron
1941 - 1945
Famous Commonwealth Squadrons of WW2
No.453 (R.A.A.F.) Squadron
1941-1945
Buffalo, Spitfire
ALLIED WINGS
ALLIED WINGS